BIBLICAL
PERSPECTIVES
ON AGING

OVERTURES TO BIBLICAL THEOLOGY

Editors

WALTER BRUEGGEMANN, Professor of Old Testament at Columbia Theological Seminary, Decatur, Georgia

JOHN R. DONAHUE, S.J., Professor of New Testament at the Jesuit School of Theology, Berkeley, California

*God
and
the
Elderly*

BIBLICAL
PERSPECTIVES
ON AGING

J. GORDON HARRIS

FORTRESS PRESS   Philadelphia

———————

Library of Congress Cataloging-in-Publication Data

Harris, J. Gordon.
  Biblical perspectives on aging.

  (Overtures to biblical theology; 22)
  Includes index.
  1. Aged in the Bible. 2. Aged—Near East.
3. Aged—Palestine. I. Title. II. Series.
BS680.A34H37   261.8′3426   86–46426
ISBN 0–8006–1547–6

———————

2529C87   Printed in the United States of America 1–1547

Dedicated to
Mrs. James G. (Tunis) Harris,
my mother, who lends
dignity to the word elder.

Contents

Editor's Foreword

Current discussions in biblical theology make clear that the old distinction between "what is meant" and "what it means" is no longer workable. There has been legitimated a concern for contemporaneity that was, until recently, unthinkable. That new legitimacy has come about for two reasons. First, attention to the *canon* means that the literature is not exclusively kept in "early" or "original" context, but is heard and permitted to have its say in a variety of contexts, including our own. Attention to canon has shown that this is normative literature which moves past one initial context into many other contexts. Second, then, the emergence of *contextualization* in interpretation has helped us see that texts are heard differently in different contexts, depending on circumstance, method, and interest. While *canon* and *contextualization* appear to go in antithetical directions, both of them together have permitted the Bible to be interpreted around fresh questions.

To be sure, there is a danger in asking questions of the text that are our questions rather than those of the text itself, but even highly disciplined critical scholarship has tended to focus on questions that are essentially alien to the text. Recent "contemporary" study appears to be more subjective than conventional "critical" study, but it is clear that in both cases the social context of scholarship has helped determine the agenda for research. There are no obviously "proper" questions to ask the text. There are only questions that arise in the process of interpretation. This is not a situation for despair as though we do not know how to proceed. Nor is it an invitation to indifference, as though any question is as good as any other. Rather it is an opportunity to focus in fresh directions that may open the text in new ways.

Professor Harris has undertaken just such an investigation around a fresh question. His book is deeply rooted in critical study and offers an amazing amount of fresh data of a historical-critical kind. But it is clear that he has not lingered on those matters. He has ranged over the entire canon and has considered texts outside the canon. It is equally clear that his question on "the elderly" is contextualized in our own social setting, in which people are living longer at the very time when old social networks of human care and valuing are less and less effective. Just when those networks are needed, they seem more and more dysfunctional. Freedom with the entire canon and freshness from context characterize this study.

One way in which biblical theology is now pursued is by sustained consideration of a single theme throughout the Bible. The Overtures to Biblical Theology series has done this in a number of cases including blessing (Westermann), death (Bailey), possessions (Johnson), suffering of God (Fretheim), faithfulness (Sakenfeld), and land (Brueggemann). In some ways, Harris continues that enterprise. However, he has addressed a more difficult problem, because his theme is not explicit in the Bible, and we may imagine that the Bible itself had no direct interest in the question of the elderly, as it did, for example, with questions of land, death, and faithfulness. This has made Harris's task more difficult and required him to be more discerning. He has had to draw his conclusions on rather indirect and unintentional evidence.

Dealing with the theme of the elderly has posed an additional problem. It is not always easy to distinguish what is theologically intentional in the Bible and what is sociologically taken for granted. At some points the Bible is surely intentional in its theological concern about the elderly, as in the fifth commandment of the decalogue. But at many other points, the Bible appropriates and practices what is common in ancient Near Eastern culture, and it likely does so without great intentionality or reflectiveness. Harris has not been able to sort out such matters in every case, nor can anyone. It is surely the case that Israel's theological intentionality is not in a vacuum, but is rooted in and shaped by a social experience and partakes both of commonality and of peculiarity. The convergence of social practice and theological intent gives a view of the elderly that is rooted in social actuality. In our interpretation we can learn much from the social actuality of Israel and the early church which is so unlike our own social reality and which may provide a place from which to criticize and transform our own social practice. The very unlikeness of situations may be especially suggestive for our fresh perception of our own situation.

I suggest Harris has dealt with three difficult problems. First, he has considered Israel's teaching and practice in relation to the elderly which is largely implicit and unintentional. Second, he has dealt with a combination of sociology and theology, which are closely intertwined with each other. Third, he has written an essay on social ethics. Scholarship has found it exceedingly difficult to find adequate categories through which to deal with ethical dimensions of biblical faith. Either one ends with making general statements about justice and love, or one deals with individual texts. While both of these procedures are important, Harris has provided an important attempt at ethics that concerns social process, social practice, and social value. Thus his work is important for its address of this difficult question of method.

Finally, I commend the book because of its obvious pertinence in our own social situation. The crisis of the elderly in contemporary society is urgent. It would be easy to conclude that our social situation is so different from that of the Bible that the Bible is not of primary use. However, insofar as the Bible is taken as a source for social visioning (which is not to say an answer book), it is important to ask what the Bible tells us on this pressing matter. Harris has provided the most complete and detailed statement we have on these matters. It is clear that ancient sociological practices of "what it meant" still now "mean" something. That meaning is not easily accessible but Harris has gone a long way in showing us our path into and through the material. I anticipate that this book will be an important reference and resource for those who seek linkages between this old text, old caring social practice, and a new question for which we are scarcely prepared.

WALTER BRUEGGEMANN
Columbia Theological Seminary
October 1, 1986

Preface

Biblical Perspectives on Aging represents the end result of a long pilgrimage that began in 1979 with an essay delivered to gerontologists on "The Bible and Aging." Research on this book, however, began in earnest during a sabbatical at the University of Heidelberg in 1982. Professor Rolf Rendtorff, who served as my host, and Professor Rainer Albertz encouraged and enriched my efforts with their grasp of interdisciplinary issues and continental scholarship, their sincere friendship, and their gracious hospitality. Students at North American Baptist Seminary interacted with an initial draft, and colleagues patiently read subsequent manuscripts and made helpful suggestions. Special commendations go to professors Tom Johnson and Michael Hagan for their contributions.

Though scholars and students in the fields of Bible and gerontology will find this work especially valuable, leaders of churches and synagogues who seek guidance from the Bible on issues of aging will also find the work stimulating. It challenges members of Christianity and Judaism to rediscover the roots of their society, ethics, and theology. It is the desire of the author that because of this book many more people may age with dignity and a sense of worth in an environment more sensitive to their needs.

Additional words of gratitude are due my spouse, Joyce, and our daughters, Joy and Jami. They have shown patience and support during the research and writing of the book. Rita Jerke deserves special recognition for her careful typing of the manuscript through its many revisions.

Bible translations, unless otherwise noted, are the work of the author. Inclusive language has been used where possible. Translations of proverbs are influenced by William McKane, *Proverbs: A New Approach,* Old Testament Library (Philadelphia: Westminster Press, 1970). In respect for Jewish preference, the divine name normally is translated as "Lord." Jewish readers who desire more information on the subject of respect for parents in their tradition may consult Gerald Blidstein, *Honor Thy Father and Mother* (New York: Ktav, 1978).

Clarifications for translations of texts from the ancient Near East are placed in parentheses; restorations of missing sections appear in brackets.

J. GORDON HARRIS
Sioux Falls, South Dakota

Introduction

Why write a book about God and the elderly? Sociologists study the structural effects of an aging America, but should theologians? Gerontologists evaluate problems and seek solutions to the dilemmas of aging, but should the church? Politicians consider financial options for future Social Security programs, but what have these concerns to do with the Bible? Psychologists and medical doctors treat the mental and physical problems of the elderly, but in these matters what role can biblical theology play? Until now, many secular groups have acted as advocates for the elderly and opposed ageism. Why change?

First, despite many advocacy efforts of concerned citizens, the public is still generally indifferent toward aging issues. Society needs additional pressure to facilitate change. Religion appears to be a proper vehicle for enlightening public opinion, confronting society's attitudes, and encouraging the elderly themselves.[1] The Bible could and should assume a pivotal role in influencing future trends. Unfortunately, some religious leaders unconsciously encourage ageism by misinterpreting difficult passages and by overlooking elderly heroes in certain biblical events. It is important that biblical theology begin to clarify such unfortunate distortions.

A second reason for writing a book on God and the elderly comes from a concern for that growing percentage of the population—the aging—who daily encounter increasing hostility in the Western world. For instance, the population of North America and Europe continues to age. In 1879 about 1.2 million people in the United States, comprising about 3 percent of the population, were over sixty-five years old. By 1900 3.1 million elderly made up 4.1 percent of the nation. By 1960 the number of elderly had reached 16.7 million, 1970, 20 million, and by 1980 25.5 million.[2] This final figure represents 11.3 percent of the population or approximately one in every nine persons. The percentage of older persons increased between 1970 and 1980 by 28 percent. By the year 2000, persons sixty-five and older are expected to represent 13.1 percent and by 2030 approximately 21.1 percent of the population.[3] The percentage of persons sixty-five and older in many countries in Europe is already surpassing that of the United States.[4] For the sake of this growing minority the resources of faith need to be marshaled.

What makes society feel uncomfortable with aging issues is that every member of the human race ages daily. That feeling remains despite dramatic medical advances that increase everyone's chances for living past sixty-five. Infants born today generally will live about twenty-six years longer than a child born in 1900. A child born in 1980 in the United States on the average will live 73.6 years. Persons reaching age sixty-five in 1980 may expect an additional 16.4 years. Physical and social problems caused by longevity reach beyond the capabilities of current social remedies whether they be social security, medicare, or any other government program. No new meaningful role or social structure in the Western world has emerged capable of carrying the weight of an aging population.

Competition between generations compounds aging dilemmas and threatens existing social structures. For instance, governmental debate of new tax programs brings out hostility and fear. Younger employed persons oppose increases in pensions and social security payments because they fear increased taxes. In the dispute, the elderly feel targeted as political scapegoats. Intergenerational debate heats up as people realize the limitations placed on resources.

Adequate medical care for the elderly also remains a difficult and emotional issue to solve. Extremes in medical treatment further complicate the discussion. At times good medical care may be denied older patients who "might die anyway." In other situations physicians overutilize hospitals and the most expensive components of medical care. The magnitude of medical costs associated with the last year of life and long-term health care may become catastrophic. The absence of a program to finance long-term maintenance of persons with chronic functional impairments penalizes elderly living near the poverty line and those who have adequate financial resources.[5]

The elderly themselves ultimately suffer most as victims of negative stereotypes about old age. When society demeans them because they are old or shows "ageism," it robs them of a sense of worth. When businesses gauge productivity by long work weeks and subsequent financial contributions, the retired obviously feel discriminated against. Mandatory retirement policies and government regulations allow few healthy retirees to supplement inadequate pensions or to continue working if they so choose. Many retire to experience uselessness and, finally, death.

Religion offers a legitimate context for dialogue between the theological tenets of biblical materials and current sociological structures. As prophets addressed crises of their society, so their messages remain capable of dialoguing anew with current abuses. Theologians must challenge the presuppositions of ageism on biblical grounds; then members of churches and synagogues may listen sympathetically to descriptions of the elderly's plight. Ancient, family-oriented societies offer helpful correctives for a throwaway, futuristic culture.

THE NATURE OF GOD AND AGING ISSUES

Before constructive dialogue can occur between biblical theology and current attitudes toward growing older, religious leaders need to examine the nature of God in light of aging experiences. A careful analysis of the divine being in light of previously noted aging concerns presents a somewhat distinctive picture of God. "Aging" emphases do not replace other aspects of the divine nature; rather, they isolate those that would be most meaningful to older persons. Though no absolute order can be established, three important biblical aspects of God might be stated as:

1. God the agent of blessing
2. God the protector of social structures
3. God the proponent of justice

God the Agent of Blessing

Biblical theology and teaching remain dominated by an event-centered image of God as deliverer. Such an emphasis neglects the equally important contiguous activity of God as the one who blesses.

Claus Westermann terms this an "error that led Western theology to a number of further misinterpretations of and deviation from the message of the Bible."[6] The reversal of this one-dimensional view of God bodes well for a biblical dialogue with aging issues. A broadening of the concept of God as one who performs mighty acts to a concept including God as one who provides the elements of growth and happiness offers aging adults clear benefits.[7]

Before the benefits of divine blessing can be analyzed, however, the meaning of blessing needs to be clarified. It needs to be separated from the earlier, magical form of the patriarchal blessings and Balaam's blessing of Israel (Numbers 23). This form relies on a charismatic person or power to determine the future. Such a blessing does not magically lead the aging into a blissful old age.

Likewise, a divine blessing for the elderly may not depend upon the righteousness demanded in the contractual terminology of Deuteronomy or on the conditions set forth in wisdom literature. In a world of medical technology righteousness alone does not lengthen life. Also, lengthened life, success, and wealth do not automatically make old age a happy and fulfilling time of life.

Even the priestly blessing does not adequately express the full meaning of divine blessing (e.g., Genesis 1, Numbers 6). While it is unconditional, it nevertheless meets institutional needs and can become an empty ritual. Divine blessing assumes these historical contexts and forms and yet represents much more.

Divine blessing in its full significance provides all generations with the power and conditions to grow vertically: to move through childhood, maturation, and physical decline in a state of being blessed.[8] Such a description of blessing opens for the elderly a new sense of worth and a propensity toward growth.

Through divine blessing God provides the essential elements for growth. Recognition of these elements may restore hope and dignity to the aging. These conditions insure that an aging body holds the potential for self-fulfillment and happiness. Salvation represents more than deliverance. It includes also a state of being blessed. This sense of security and continuity calms fears associated with the mystery and unknowns of aging.

God the Protector of Social Structures

Biblical traditions about creation, election, and Royal-Zion theology teach that the structure of society finds its origins and continuity with the will of God. Such a view undergirds an ordered sense of living that affirms divine providence. God both establishes a system of relationships and asserts sovereignty over it. In this way the kingdom of heaven legitimates and preserves worthy earthly structures and social arrangements.[9]

Structural legitimation serves the ruling class, but it also provides a supportive system for the elderly. The granting of honor to otherwise vulnerable parents and aging leaders depends on the preservation of order and respect. In this way, the Lord (Yahweh) and Israel are yoked together in a "common theology" and walking toward common goals. When this system comes into jeopardy because of sociopolitical shifts as well as religious apathy, God acts to assert in stronger terms crucial elements of that social structure that need to be regained and solidified.

Though God seems to promote a system as an acceptable solution, the powerful should not view this common theology as a legitimation of their particular sociopolitical point of view or methods. Israel's God retains a certain freedom to accept or reject such on the basis of contractual standards. God does not sanction unconditionally the practices of any particular ruler or structure. God acts as an enforcer of order and respect but at the same time expresses indignation when a structure falls short of its contractual ideals.

Aging citizens may discover a measure of comfort in the support offered by their creator and sovereign. God promises continuity and does not abandon those who grow old (implied in the petition of an older worshiper in Ps. 71:9, 18 and the assurance of being heard in vv. 19–21). They retain worth as a result of an orderly creation and as recipients of honor and respect. Aging citizens within the people of God experience support and comfort by realizing that their God protects their status in an appropriate, consistent, and personal manner.

God as Proponent of Justice

A third statement about God seems to conflict with the first two characteristics. God as the proponent of justice often clashes with the role of structure legitimation. Justice as a divine category suggests that God sides with a fragile minority against a blessed, powerful, but oppressive structure. In this sense God acts as deliverer of the weak, provides blessing for the neglected and protection for the powerless. These divine tenets seem to contradict those of the common theology.

In the justice of God, however, the aging also find comfort and hope. God the deliverer angrily rejects those who exploit those of diminished status. Since aging implies an eventual weakening of the physical, social, and economic powers of an older person, the elderly may depend increasingly on God's protection from enemies both within the family and from the outside. God's deliverance from self-serving structures and persons may enable the elderly to assume their rightful role as elders or leaders. An exodus from a fate similar to slavery and uselessness on a personal and social scale may occur daily through divine commitment to justice. Such a commitment ultimately supplies the aging with the necessary confidence and hope to face death.

All three aspects of God appear in complex traditions and forms, scattered throughout the Scriptures. Israel's common theology of divine blessing and protection of social structures does not remain static. The Bible describes appropriate variations, social interaction, and numerous reactions to changing historical situations. At times Israel's relationship with God enriches in unique ways ancient Near Eastern views of the elderly. In most instances, the God of Israel promotes an environment of growth and freedom in which all generations can discover the joy of living in mutual respect and interdependence. These teachings need to dialogue with aging issues in a fresh way.

THE BIBLE AND AGING ISSUES: A CROSS-DISCIPLINARY APPROACH

Normally an investigation of social issues in the Bible confronts a serious shortage of data. The Bible lacks a systematic theology of aging and a comprehensive account of the treatment of elders. Instead clues about general attitudes and practices must be gleaned from a careful cross-disciplinary study of biblical literature itself. Such materials must be interpreted in the perspective of anthropological evidence from surrounding cultures and their related literatures.

The Use of Anthropological Evidence

Relative lack of biblical evidence makes a careful study of the anthropological and social materials from related cultures an important task. Comparative evidence demonstrates the complexity of ancient social institutions. It provides an extensive background for interpreting biblical evidence. It should not lead to simplistic conclusions or restrictive correlations between cultures.

On the other hand, a systematic examination of literary data within its particular context can illumine the interpretation of limited biblical data. The work follows several guidelines to guard against methodological errors.[10] (1) Anthropological data is collected from sources that generally are reliable even though they are secondary works. The collection of data attempts to be as systematic and as thorough as limitations allow. (2) Generalizations are based on interpreting comparative data within its own social and historical context. (3) Social data from the ancient Near East is interpreted in light of a survey of literatures from a wide range of societies. (4) Though data collected will never be complete and hence its conclusions will be somewhat tentative, it is selected for this work as that which relates best to aging issues in biblical evidence. (5) The biblical text ever remains the primary factor in utilizing comparative data. In instances where the Bible possesses insufficient corroborative evidence, the author will treat as tentative an interpretation based on comparative materials.

Incorporating comparative anthropological evidence into the discussion enhances the recognition of biblical attitudes and establishes a basis for determining the nature of a common theology of aging in the ancient Near East. Likewise, the data provides grounds for isolating unique contributions of Israel's traditions. This evidence, therefore, supplements in a helpful way the paucity of social data in the Bible.

Interpreting the Bible in Light of Aging Issues

The study of biblical material has to take into account the complexity of Israel's traditions. Information about the elderly appears in a variety of literary forms and is the product of a long period of development. Though the nature of this work limits the number of linguistic, historical, and literary comments that can be included, it makes an effort to take into account the general literary contexts and historical milieu of passages.

Only crucial passages are examined in detail. Others are surveyed. The survey method allows more of the evidence to be treated and allows certain texts which frequently are ignored or misunderstood to be reinterpreted. A general outline of the history of attitudes and practices toward the elderly emerges from the survey. The in-depth study of a few important passages allows the work to consider the complexity of tradition (e.g., the Ten Commandments). However, concentration on a few texts necessarily limits the conclusions that can be drawn about the materials.

The interpretation of texts from a hermeneutical viewpoint, taking into account aging concerns, assumes the validity of a theology of aging.[11] It calls for taking into account the increased significance of aging in human experience. It recognizes in aging potential contributions to theological understanding. It opens the Scriptures to a more pluralistic and inclusive methodology which also probes into the aging experience.

Such a methodology, however, must not be used uncritically. It must take carefully into account the ancient context of a passage and its primary intent. Nevertheless, that passage may need to deal with new issues in light of current attitudes toward that which is old and toward aging in general. In this case secondary concerns may need to be examined before the primary thrust of a passage can be interpreted in an inclusive manner. The book does not call for a gray theology as much as it attempts to sensitize readers to take into account the aging experience when interpreting biblical materials.

BIBLICAL THEOLOGY AND AGING ISSUES

Recent publications indicate that religion and gerontology already are reuniting.[12] This work attempts to broaden that dialogue to include biblical studies. Responsibility demands that these disciplines enter the dialogue with religion and gerontology.

Biblical theology continues to seek a method that takes into account the diversity and unity of the Bible. This method must relate to social structures and concerns if it is to inquire into the aging experience. It also must allow for historical development and literary complexity.

One such method is proposed by Walter Brueggemann.[13] He recognizes within the work of the deity a certain amount of "structure legitimation." Such concerns for legitimation of the social order are shared by Israel and its neighbors. One might call this a "common theology." Divine power reinforces the structures of society, perpetuating order and security. This common theology provides the basic structure for respect of the elderly in the biblical data. Hence, this methodology is especially attractive to a study of the Bible and aging issues.

On the other hand, determining when and how biblical instruction departs from social legitimation to describe God as one who uniquely relates to the experiences of the aging is more difficult than isolating the common theology. Yet the description of the unique relationship between God and the aging in the Bible allows Christians and Jews to understand better how their deity blesses and delivers those facing old age.

Despite the tentative nature of choosing criteria for isolating different theologies, the method facilitates the organization of data into a history of Israel's instruction and practices relating to the elderly. It allows the author to deal with both the diversity and unity of biblical teachings concerning aging. It also takes into account social concerns that influence directly a theology of aging. The method clarifies how God can be the agent of blessing, the protector of social structures, and at the same time a proponent of justice. It helps explain how God challenges the elderly to growth and at the same time provides the basic elements for growth. It takes into account both continuity and change within the actions of God.

As a prototype for a dialogue between biblical data and gerontology, this book examines biblical attitudes and practices that relate to current aging experiences. Without claiming to be comprehensive, the book presents representative elements of a dialogue on aging that developed within Israel's experiences and faith. Chapter 1 defines the issues of aging and how the Bible and its related literatures described old age. Chapter 2 outlines what the literatures of the ancient Near

East teach about aging and intergenerational relationships. Chapter 3 highlights values Israel shared with its neighbors, which may be termed a common theology on aging.

Chapter 4 describes common tensions and seeds of ambiguity that limit the implementing of Israel's values and attitudes toward the elder generation. Discussions in chapter 5 present the unique emphases and concerns of Israel's variations on this common theology. Chapter 6 covers the responses of two great faiths, Christianity and Judaism, to various mandates of respect for the elderly. Finally, Chapter 7 applies these biblical concerns to present Western attitudes and practices. Such an approach examines biblical data through the lenses of the experiences of aging.

Adherents to Christianity and Judaism[14] will journey in this book to the roots of their heritage and begin there to probe the significance of aging. Both faiths proclaim honor and respect for the elderly. An aging population in the Western world requires that both utilize their moral and religious resources to help shape the future. This work presents evidence and perspectives that may enable both to respond redemptively to crises attendant to that new age.

CHAPTER 1

Aging Experiences
and the Bible

The interpretation of texts in light of the significance of aging in human experience assumes that old age can be defined. That is more difficult than at first it seems. Modern physicians cannot define old age precisely. Individuals age physically and socially at different rates. Demographics currently use the age of sixty-five as a reference point for retirement and therefore old age. However, records from earlier generations list shorter life spans and future inhabitants may extend life expectancy considerably. Determining old age remains as elusive as ever.

On the other hand, certain physical and social characteristics always are associated with old age. Although that period of life now often extends some thirty years and may be divided into the young old (sixty-five to seventy-four), the middle old (seventy-five to eighty-four), and the older old (eighty-five and older), several constants remain in that experience. These characteristics form the basis for describing the aging experience as it appears in the Bible and the ancient Near East.[1]

PHYSICAL CHARACTERISTICS OF OLD AGE

Words describing common physical characteristics of maturity indicate the arrival of old age. Languages throughout the ancient Near East use "white hair" (wool)[2] to designate one of optimum age and wisdom. White hair in all cultures represents the most common characteristic of old age.

A second word, "elder," refers to another common characteristic of one who has attained maturity and leadership.[3] The Hebrew cognate associates this stage of life with the time when a man could grow a beard. Since men and women were betrothed at an early age in ancient oriental societies, the ability of a male to produce a beard— not marriage itself—initiates for the male the transition from youth to full responsibility. Though hypothetically an elder was any person past puberty, the term usually indicates older persons holding leadership positions. In different instances, it designates a clan leader, a local official, and an old person. Its feminine form also describes older women. The word normally indicates older persons, heads of family.

CHRONOLOGICAL AGE AND OLD AGE

A varied vocabulary indicates advanced chronological age. Some ancient texts record a person's specific age. Idioms describe longevity as "full of days" or "advanced in years."[4] Long life in the ancient literatures represents an exceptional achievement. People view advanced years as a special indication of a person's importance (Gen. 5:1–32) and as a sign of divine favor.[5] Exceptions to this rule do appear and the Bible notes one with an explanation, mentioning Enoch who walked with God and yet lived a relatively short time. The text briefly explains his demise by saying, "God took him" (Gen. 5:22–24).

The Bible glorifies some of its heroes by reciting their exceptional longevity. For example, a Deuteronomic summary praises the good health of Moses at his death (Deut. 34:7), and Caleb brags about his extra vigor at eighty-five years of age (Josh. 14:10–11). Though the nature and dates of such passages vary, traditions of Israel glorify clan heroes by attributing to them legendary life spans and exceptional health. Such reports enhance their reputations.

A study of fourteen kings from the dynasty of David presents a clearer picture of the average life span during the royal eras of Israel, 926–597 B.C.E.[6] Omitting Jehoiachim, Jehoiachin, and Zedekiah, the age at death of the remaining kings ranged from sixty-six (Manasseh) to twenty-one (Ahaziah). Their age at death averages forty-four. Assuming that rulers enjoyed a diet and medical care superior to that of an average Israelite, it is clear that few persons enjoyed a life of seventy or eighty years (contra Ps. 90:10).

After Moses (120 years), only Joshua (110), Job (140), and the High Priest Jehoida (130, 2 Chron. 24:15) are said to surpass one hundred. Only in the eschatological kingdom could people hope to attain an extended life span such as one hundred years (Isa. 65:20). Generally, old age could begin earlier than age sixty-five.

TRANSITIONS OF LIFE AND OLD AGE

The Bible also describes the aging experience as a sequence of the seasons of life. Such seasons indicate common transitions in life: childhood, youth, maturity/elderly.[7] Life also is pictured as four seasons: childhood, youth, young marrieds, elderly (Jer. 51:22); or five stages: small child, youth (maturity begins at age thirteen, Gen. 17:25), adult men and women, elderly *(zaqen),* and aged *(mele' yamim)* (Jer. 6:11).

Life's transitions indicate changes in the work and role patterns of individuals. A twenty-year-old male would be considered responsible as an adult (Num. 14:29; 32:11) and therefore liable to enter military service (Num. 1:3, 18; 26:2; 2 Chron. 25:5) and to pay taxes (Exod. 30:14). Levites are said to actively work as priests between ages thirty (Num. 4:3, Kohathites; twenty-five, Levites, Num. 8:24)[8] and fifty. After age fifty they retire to assist the younger priests (Num. 8:24–26). Zechariah, the father of John the Baptist, considered his wife and himself "old" and yet he served in the temple (Luke 1:18–25). Age fifty during biblical eras might be termed a "ripe, old age." Though little is known directly about other occupations, they may have followed a similar retirement pattern, though the age of transition obviously varied with the type of work performed.

Life transitions are somewhat different in agricultural occupations. Agricultural work is so difficult that parents may have retired from active farming as soon as the children were old enough to work in the fields. However, after retirement in Israel parents do not cease to lead the clan. Both parents now enjoy the luxury of time and energy for training grandchildren and advising the younger generation. Certainly a father or mother might also work as an elder or judge for the clan, the community, and in some cases a tribe or nation.

Payments for vows (Leviticus 27)[9] provide estimates expressing official comparative values for men and women at different stages of life. Though the amounts of money may have varied with different periods of history, they represent ways people could complete vows in the temple or pay fines to redeem difficult personal vows. Prices may represent the cost of a slave at that age in life.[10] The peak value for a male (twenty to sixty years) may represent that time when he could be conscripted (twenty years and over) for military service as indicated by census instructions (cf. Num. 1:3, 20, 22; 26:2, 4; 2 Chron. 25:5). Payments could vary if the votary claimed poverty. Nevertheless, these figures do provide a glimpse into how Israelites valued life in its transitions. Such evaluations indicate the worth of a person's contribution to the life of a community in terms of work capacity.

	male	female
1 mo.–5 yrs. old	5	3 (shekels)
		(pieces of silver)
5 yrs.–20 yrs. old	20	10
20 yrs.–60 yrs. old	50	30
More than 60	15	10

Lev. 27:1–8

Though certainly the value of a male child and adult always remains higher than that of a female, some equalization eventually emerges. In old age the value of an older woman does not drop as much as that of an older man. The comparative worth of the older woman changes from the earlier ratio of three to five to that of two to three. Such changes may indicate that elderly women lived healthier and more active lives than men. The drop in value of both genders at age sixty may indicate that by that age both retired from public service and entered the season of old age.

PHYSICAL LOSS AND OLD AGE

The Bible also mentions several physical losses that accompany old age. A key transition for the woman comes at menopause, when she loses the ability to give birth to children. When a woman could no longer give birth (Gen. 18:11; Ruth 1:12; Luke 1:18, 36–37) or a man was thought too old to produce a child for his wife (Gen. 18:12), that person was considered old. Failing health (e.g., loss of hearing, sight, or normal vigor) also indicates old age (Gen. 27:1–2).

To some degree old age brings a loss of income as well as signifi-

cance. Women especially experience this dilemma. Widows in the
Bible represent the most traumatic examples of those who are helpless and worthy of support from the community. They lose more than
a husband. Biblical laws and prophets often link them with the
orphan or fatherless. Countless examples could be cited of widows
who suffered severe deprivation. Ruth and Naomi, for example,
struggle with no male support to find a measure of security in the
house of a kinsman-redeemer. Without a kinsman-redeemer or sympathy from a godly leader, widows of all ages possess little hope
(1 Kings 17:9–24; 2 Kings 4:1–7). Consequently, the "reproach of
widowhood" remains synonymous with suffering and loss (Isa. 54:4;
Lam. 1:1; 5:3–4; Rev. 18:7).

Admittedly not every widow in the Bible is elderly. Some, like
Ruth, become widows at a young age and frequently remarry. On the
other hand, older widows such as Naomi, who hold no hope of
remarriage, become particularly vulnerable. They must depend on
protection from adult children and/or society. The older widow often
experiences deep bitterness and depression because of her severe
losses (Ruth 1:20–21). Therefore biblical texts single out older widows as the afflicted in need of extra help and compassion (1 Tim.
5:3–8).[11]

The Bible reveals the God of Israel as the defender of powerless
widows (Deut. 10:18). For this reason God commands the people of
the covenant to care for such (Deut. 14:29; 24:17, 19–21). When
people fail to fulfill their responsibilities for vulnerable members of
their society, prophets condemn their behavior (Isa. 1:23; 10:2; Mic.
2:9; Mal. 3:5), as do other writers also (Job 22:9; 24:3; 31:16; Ps.
94:6).

Aging fathers, likewise, become victims of ambitious sons in the
Bible. Witness the way Jacob manipulates his nearly blind father into
giving him the blessing that belonged to Esau (Genesis 27). Note also
the ease with which Absalom nearly overthrows his aging father
David the king. Leaders in Hebron, themselves former supporters of
David, join with Absalom in the plot. Only youthful foolishness
keeps it from succeeding (2 Samuel 15—19).

Prophets condemn disregard for vulnerable parents (Mic. 7:6).
Intergenerational love remains their ideal (Mal. 4:6). Still, such warnings indicate that some adult children took advantage of aging parents

who suffered some loss of strength and independence in life's transitions. Christianity shares this concern by mentioning that Jesus condemns those who shirk the care of aging parents through a religious vow called "Corban" (Mark 7:5–13).

Aging parents in the ancient Near East enter a somewhat dependent and vulnerable stage of life when they become elderly. Therefore, old age in the Bible signifies the transition into a weakened social and physical condition. That transition remains a reliable basis for examining experiences of old age in the Bible.

SUMMARY

While the experience of aging in the Bible defies precise definition, the materials mention traits that distinguish that season from other periods of life. White hair most often indicated aging. As well, community or clan leadership identified as eldership was reserved for the older person. Elder status may have begun as early as thirty or forty years of age.

Often the Bible described aging by referring to life's transitions. A person's value for work changed with age. When a marriage partner passed the age for giving birth to children or a spouse could no longer bring about offspring, they were said to be old. Clearly, persons reached old age when in life's later stages they experienced failing health and infirmities. The helplessness of widowhood made a woman more vulnerable to aging than her male counterpart. At times the transitions to old age for both sexes brought encroaching weakness with a lowering of production and status.

In recognition of these factors of aging, it is not surprising that the God of Israel supported an elevated status for the elderly and reinforced their claims to sustenance and respect. God by nature sought to protect the vulnerable. God did this both by supporting order in society and by responding to violations of its contractual ideals in angry words and actions.

Chapter 2 collates some disparate teachings about intergenerational relations preserved in the extant literature of the ancient Near East. This collection of anecdotes clarifies the origin of many biblical values concerning the elderly. Quotations about intergenerational relationships appear scattered throughout various types of literature and in widely different historical contexts. Still, a general pattern does emerge from which an outline may be structured for determining the background of Israel's "common theology" of aging. This collection aids in the isolating of biblical themes on aging, those generally accepted in the ancient Near East as well as Israel's distinctive variants.

CHAPTER 2

Attitudes Toward
the Elderly in the
Ancient Near East

A Common Theology

Respect for older persons appears to be accepted universally in the remnants of the literature of the ancient Near East. Such behavior helps stabilize and preserve social structures. Even the gods are said to reinforce the norms of society and hence the power and needs of older citizens. A consolidation of these views provides the assumptions for the social and theological beliefs of a common theology on aging.

A common theology of aging for the ancient Near East may be derived from legal sanctions which generally support those in power and from religious texts which provide the necessary mythology for elevating the status quo. These materials demonstrate how religious practices secure obedience and honor for those in power. Divinely ordained statutes reinforce submission to authority and perpetuate religious and political bureaucracies. In a similar fashion, divine support for the rights and privileges of prominent older citizens guarantees their control over younger generations. Agents of the status quo fear the temperament and strength of youth and youth's potential to breed anarchy. Hence, respect for elders becomes for them a significant factor for maintaining a stable society. Such concerns motivate the formation of a common theology on aging.

A statement that assumes that ancient oriental ideals on aging serve only to legitimate structural interests would be entirely too simplistic. Such teachings reflect a concern for the welfare of aging parents and admiration for their contributions to society. Though sanctions normally secure the interests of the powerful, ancient oriental statutes also protect vulnerable aging citizens and elevate their wisdom over that of bureaucrats. These ideals legitimate structures that enhance the roles of the elderly and their positions as representatives of the past and advisers to the young.

MESOPOTAMIA: RESPECT REINFORCES AUTHORITY

Extant literary remains from ancient city-states of Mesopotamia preserve statutes, proverbs, and myths that protect the stability of their societies and show that support for the authority of prominent leaders was given for geographical, social, and religious reasons.

For example, tablets from first millennium B.C.E. describe life in Mesopotamia as insecure. Flooding woes caused by the Tigris and Euphrates rivers, together with chaotic city-state rivalry, created a climate of uncertainty about the future. Even ancient Mesopotamian gods are said to delight in capricious and unpredictable behavior. In times of turmoil weak pilgrims struggle to survive this hostile environment.

> They (gods or people?) strengthen the mighty man, whose retinue is (wickedness). (But) they ruin the weakling, they cast down the feeble. (*ANET*, 440)[1]

Under these conditions the future remains uncertain. Hope for survival of the average person depends on obedience to the gods and their subsequent support of social structures. Therefore, ancient Mesopotamian laws on intergenerational relationships generally reinforce order and authority in society.[2]

Society in this context strengthens its rings of authority by calling for the younger to obey the older members. Younger children are required to obey older brothers and sisters, parents, and authorities. These commands are reinforced by threats of disinheritance. Since parents hold an almost absolute authority over the estate, such threats increase pressure on the younger generation to submit.

Respect for the Elderly Reinforced by Threats

Mesopotamian laws and statutes further reinforce obedience of parents by threatening children with severe penalties. The Code of

Hammurabi, composed between 1728 and 1686 B.C.E., records unique insights into Mesopotamian life, manners, and society. The severity of its threatened penalties underlines how seriously the culture viewed filial offenses against parents:

> If a man strikes his father, they shall cut off his forehand. (*ANET,* 175)
>
> An adopted son who leaves the house of his adopted parents to return to his natural father's house, one shall pluck out his eye. An adopted son who says to one who brought him up "You are not my Father, you are not my Mother," one shall cut out his tongue. (*ANET,* 175)[3]

Similar laws from *ana ittishu,* a school workbook, warn:

> A son who says: "You are not my Father," shave his head, put the mark of a slave on him and sell him.
>
> A son who says to his mother: "You are not my mother!" Shave half of his head and lead him round the city and put him out of the house.[4]

Such commands obviously threaten responsible children who fail to respect their parents.

Social legislation associated with Hammurabi especially singles out the vulnerable widow for special protection. Ungrateful adult sons easily could abuse and neglect their mother. Consequently, justice demands that sons not evict their widowed mother from property even when the land belongs to them. Sons are forbidden from "making a claim against her." That statute is strengthened by inheritance laws that state that a mother could give her estate to the one whom she loved.[5]

Middle Assyrian laws also support the widowed mother (*ANET,* 173). One law states that even when her husband has left no will, her sons are to care for their mother as "one would a bride" with food and drink. Even early Sumerian laws show deep compassion for one whose plight was as vulnerable as that stated in a proverb: "Selflessness (is) the widow's (lot)."[6]

Though divine sanctions protect the rights of parents, laws in ancient Mesopotamia in no way support only the parents. Parents do not own their children as cattle without rights. The Code of Hammurabi forbids disinheriting a son without at least granting him a hearing before the judges (*ANET,* 173). A child's first offense against parents could be pardoned; only a second offense might bring disinheritance.[7] To this degree Hammurabi legislation in Mesopotamia provides protection for both parents and children.

Mutual support of the generations is the ultimate goal of Mesopotamian laws as recorded in the prologue to the code of Lipit-Ishtar of Ur antedating the Code of Hammurabi by more than a century and a half:

> I made the father *support* his children (and I) made the children (support their) father; I made the father sta[nd by his] children (and) I made the children *stand by* their father. (*ANET*, 159)

Middle Assyrian wisdom literature teaches that selling one's children to pay debts is a sign of weakness:

> The strong man lives off what is paid for his strength (lit., arm) and the weak man off what is paid for his children.[8]

It is warranted only to ward off starvation.

Legal threats remain an important social tool in Mesopotamia for creating respect and for supporting stability. Individual sentences generally sustain justice, not injustice. Though at times these punishments may seem cruel to the modern reader, these sanctions ultimately seek to create mutual respect and support between the generations.

Care for the Elderly Reinforced
by Rewards

Religious documents in Mesopotamia teach that the good things of life depend upon the favor of the gods. Long life itself is viewed both as a gift from the gods and a reward for justice and care for parents. The extra-long lives of early kings demonstrate this. In the Shamash Hymn from the library of Asshurbanipal (668–633 B.C.E.), Shamash is said to reward a just judge with a long life:

> As for him who declines a present but nevertheless takes the part of the weak, it is pleasing to Shamash and he will prolong his life. (*ANET*, 388).[9]

Showing respect brings its own reward. Making a parent happy brings blessings to a child. "Bride, (as) you treat your mother-in-law, so will women (later) treat you" (*ANET*, 594). Therefore, a son is admonished by a Sumerian proverb: "Accept your lot (inheritance) (and) make your mother happy! Act promptly and make your god happy!"[10]

Mesopotamian laws further balance filial respect and its rewards with parental responsibilities. A father is obliged to treat and nurture a son as a valuable possession as is a son required to care for a parent.

> A poor man does not strike his son a single blow; he treasures him forever! (*ANET*, 191)

Children become literal treasures for parents because support for old age depends on them and the way they are treated.[11] The future of parents and the whole family depends on the actions of the sons: "The brothers in anger [P] have destroyed the estate of their father."[12]

In summary, divine sanctions recorded in a variety of periods but at least by the Middle Assyrian era supported respect between generations and reinforced lines of authority. Old age, when fate brought it, was said to come as a gift from a god as a reward for faithful obedience. Mesopotamian legal codes incorporated threats and promises to promote social stability and respect for aging parents. On the other hand, they tempered their penalties by emphasizing the rights and responsibilities of both parents and children. Thus Mesopotamian legal codes and proverbs provided important fundamental themes for a common theology of aging in the ancient Near East.

EGYPT: THE VALUE OF AGING
REINFORCES RESPECT

Ancient Egyptian culture places a similar value on growing older and views elderly citizens as significant commodities. Egyptian literature identifies age with wisdom and continuity and so admires old age. The society's educational materials stress the value of elders and point out the debt that the younger generation owes to parents and ancestors. Such materials provide effective support for aging citizens. In this way Egyptian culture relishes the past, values the contributions of ancestors, and exalts the elderly.

Egyptian culture seems ever oriented toward continuity and the glorification of old age because of its geography, social structure, and religious heritage. Regular flooding cycles of the Nile River together with Egypt's relative isolation from foreign enemies allowed Egyptians the luxury of stressing tranquillity and respect as the ways to prosperity. Under the life-giving blessings of the Nile its early culture developed without disruption. Hence its literature identifies older citizens with success, wisdom, and honor. Such norms flourished under the relative stability of Egypt's Old Kingdom.

Disintegration of the Old Kingdom, however, threatened the earlier environment of stability and prosperity. Feuding barons in 2280 B.C.E. interrupted it, bringing chaos and confusion in what is called the First Intermediate Period (2280–2000 B.C.E.).[13] The resulting instability initiated a period of reexamining basic values and of pondering the nature of righteousness. In spite of agony brought on by loss of the old and the chaos of a new order, Egypt does not appear to have rejected the old ways but rather grafted new ideas to them.

Associating Age with Wisdom Provides Respect

Literary remains from ancient Egypt leave little doubt that the elderly in Egypt passed through aging transitions common to every culture. Nevertheless, its beliefs remain entrenched in the idea that age represents the highest form of traditional wisdom. In Egyptian literature the older person promotes the ideas of the ancestors as ancient persons who directly recount the words of eternal gods. A son may achieve his life's goal by listening to what his father said and then surpassing the previous generation. Certainly in this way gods elevate obedient, youthful listeners.[14]

The honored position of an elderly person in Egypt is illustrated clearly in "The Instruction of Ani," a set of instructions from a father to his son composed in the New Kingdom, probably in the Eighteenth Dynasty.[15] "You should not sit when another who is older than you is standing or one who has been raised higher in rank" (*ANET*, 420). Egyptian wisdom of this later period (1300–1000 B.C.E.) teaches a humbler, more resigned and less materialistic message than earlier Egyptian books of wisdom. For example, "The Instruction of Amenem-opet"[16] (at times roughly paralleling Prov. 22:17—23:11, 24:10–12), admonishes youth to respect the possessions and person of the weak and disabled: "Guard yourself against robbing the wretched and against being puissant (overbearing) to the disabled" (*ANET*, 422). It calls for the younger to remain listeners around an older person: "Stretch not forth your hand to repel an old man, nor anticipate (steal the speech of) the aged" (*ANET*, 422). In this way "The Instruction of Amen-em-opet" reinforces respect for the elderly by identifying them with divine wisdom and by encouraging youth to be their listeners and students.

A Debt of Gratitude to Parents
Reinforces Respect

Without a sense of gratitude toward parents, children in Egypt might be tempted to reject parents as they aged. Greediness in children has always made parental care difficult to sustain. Justice for vulnerable, aging persons never comes easily. Even sympathetic Egyptians might make oppression the rule despite strong taboos and warnings. Note the concern for a widow in "The Instruction of Amen-em-opet": "Do not be greedy after (covet) a cubit of land, nor encroach upon (throw down) the boundaries of a widow" (*ANET*, 422).

Women in Egypt, both widows and mothers, depend on special protection from their offspring. Laws remind children of the debt of gratitude they owe parents, especially their mother. A mother gives birth to a child and trains that one. A child's faithfulness therefore should be motivated by a deep sense of gratitude. No child ever could repay that deep filial debt by doing good for parents. Notice "The Instruction of Ani" teaches:

> When you are a young man and take to yourself a wife and are settled in your house, set your eye on how your mother gave birth to you and all (her) bringing you up as well. Do not let her blame you, nor may she (have to) raise her hands to the god, nor may he (have to) hear her cries. (*ANET*, 421).

Egyptian gods reinforce this debt of gratitude in order to secure *ma'at* (justice) for feeble parents.

Despite a common concern for justice and respect, society, even oriental ones, always chooses whom of its aging to exalt. For instance, a satirical letter of the late Nineteenth Dynasty (end of the thirteenth century B.C.E.) mentions that Egyptians who are feeble but rich in houses and lands have no complaints. To the contrary a poor man named Ki-sepi, who "goes by on the ground unnoticed, unkempt of clothing and firmly wrapped up," was considered as "a bird passes by"—small and insignificant. One might have blown beside him and he would fall (*ANET,* 476). As has been common in every generation, ideals do not necessarily bring about consistent practice.

In summary, Egypt's stability during its Old Kingdom instilled in its culture the values of stability and a love of continuity. Since older persons represented the nearest links to the traditions of the ancestors, Egyptians considered them as the highest form of wisdom. Even the chaos of the Intermediate Period could not shake this concept.[17] Instead, wisdom literature from later periods broadened its teachings to include more concern for the weak, disabled, and vulnerable of society. Such concerns devoted themselves to achieving *ma'at* (justice) for feeble, aging parents. Such represent Egypt's finest contributions to the common theology of aging inherited by Israel.

CANAAN: SHIFTS IN VALUES UNDERMINE RESPECT

In contrast with the stability of norms in Egypt, values and practices in Canaan often seem to fluctuate. Though evidence remains sketchy even with discovery of the library at Ras Shamra,[18] literary discoveries from pre-Israelite Canaan allow some tentative conclusions to be drawn about its culture. As in Mesopotamia, survival and agricultural fertility dominate the religion of that people. However, that search at times renders the elderly expendable.

For instance, evidence that Canaanites shared in a universal appreciation of the elderly hardly appears in their Anath-Baal cycle.[19] Instead, disrespect for old age dominates. In these legends El, the ancient father-creator (Bull), appears to have diminished in value and power. He approaches the bloodthirsty goddess Anath and powerful storm god Baal as helpless and vulnerable. Despite the gray hair in El's beard, Anath threatens and coerces him to praise Baal. In this myth the younger, more virile Baal replaces El as the provider of protection and fertility.[20] The Anath-Baal cycle indicates that Canaanite religion and culture by 1400 B.C.E. devalued the older El and became essentially a youth cult.

An earlier Ugaritic text (*UT,* 52:30–76) reflects a higher appreciation for the elder El and implies positive expectations for the aging.[21] The text glorifies creator El as the prime sustainer of fertility. Some speakers in the myth wonder whether El is impotent in his old age.

The end of seven lean years and the beginning of seven fat years depend on whether El can copulate with two wives he has created. Fears subside when he completes his task and his wives give birth to seven sons. Ultimately the tablet praises El as he who inaugurates a new cycle of fat years by his virility. Such a myth indicates that an earlier era within Canaanite religion and culture elevated El and showed more respect for old age in general.

A high regard for the elderly becomes clearer in 2 *Aqhat* where the text spells out the duties of an ideal son to his father. A son provides proper funeral rites for his father, sets up the stele of his ancestral god, and takes the place of his father in the temple of Baal/El by eating his slice or portion of the sacrificial meal, patches the roof of his house, and washes his dirty clothes. He continues his father's hospitality and cares for his drunken father that he might not fall into dishonor: "Who may hold his hand when he is drunk, support him when he is filled with wine" (2 AQHT I: Col i, 11, 31–32).[22] Ugaritic proverbs echo similar positive feelings toward the aging. "Do not treat poorly the young with the old. With father and mother . . ."[23] Though such proverbs are broken and incomplete they indicate a general concern for the welfare and honor of the elderly and parents. Such ideals seem in tension with the Baal-Anath myths but reflect a common oriental theology of aging that ancient Canaan likewise accepted.

Extant Ugaritic legends and religious myths make it appear that Canaanite culture professed bipolar attitudes about growing old. The priorities of myths glorifying the aging El contradict those honoring the younger, virile Baal. One group shares in the divine reinforcement of the rights and privileges of elders. Other myths reflect a contempt for gray hair and infirmity.

Respect Breaks Down Under Monarchy

Though pre-Israelite inhabitants of Canaan shared a common Near Eastern theology of aging, their loyalty to Baal and his myths indicates that Canaanites later may have neglected its ideals.[24] What type of societal shifts could spawn a depreciation of the value of human life in general and respect for the older generation in particular? Monarchy, with its struggles for succession and its resulting bureaucracy, may have had something to do with these changes.

For example, an Ugaritic legend about Keret chronicles how a struggle for succession to the throne undermined commonly accepted values. Yassib, Keret's son, supplants his ailing father and assumes the throne when he thinks the king is dying. Keret recovers from his illness and regains the throne, much to the surprise of his son.[25] This legend illustrates how a quest for power may overwhelm respect for the older generation and the tenets of a common theology of aging.

Respect Breaks Down with Urbanization

Along with the rise of monarchy, an urban shift or the development of important city-states may also be a factor in the breakdown of earlier ideals. Canaanite literature indicates that such a shift took place in its two conflicting pictures of life. An older picture from Canaanite myths and legends describes a heroic age exemplifying the ideals of a tribal people led by El and his son. Elders in the town share power with the king. Occupations generally remain agricultural; there are some artisan workers. Most of life centers on the family. A son cares for the needs of his father and then carries the name and honor of his deceased ancestor.[26] Urbanization of this agrarian life style generally undermines these values and practices.

A more developed urban life style appears in Canaanite administrative documents. Akkadian letters found at Tell-el-Amarna[27] demonstrate how subjugated were the inhabitants of the countryside compared to those of the cities and their ruling class in pre-Israelite Canaan. Administrative documents from Ras Shamra[28] portray a society dominated by hereditary guilds and professional bureaucrats. Kings and generals lead armies to war. Priests conduct rites. Scribes and administrators run the economy. Districts develop for taxing the people. Large contingents of mercenary soldiers fight the wars. The king theoretically owns all the land and distributes parcels as "fiefs" to his subjects. Though evidence remains incomplete, it points toward control by the elite and diminishing power for the assemblies of free citizens or elders as a result of the concentration of population in and around cities. Documents that remain point to a centralized superstructure which impoverished the vulnerable and threatened the existence of a class of "free" peasants.[29]

Early Canaanite literature preserves examples that indicate Canaan also accepted the universal values for a common theology of aging.

Documents teach concern for the poor, elderly, and parents. However, developments in monarchy and urbanization described in administrative letters and documents from the Amarna Age indicate an increasing bureaucracy and depersonalization of society in pre-Israelite Canaan. Evidence suggests that many traditional structures broke down under pressure from these societal shifts. The breakdown of these traditional structures seems to have endangered the political and religious coalition that secures the welfare of the elderly. This also undermines the value system of a common theology of aging and makes impossible its implementation.

CONCLUSION

Throughout the literature of the ancient Near East all cultures honored the elderly in theory. To some degree these common ideals came from a desire to reinforce order and justice in society, on the one hand, and, on the other, feelings of gratitude for parents who in cooperation with the gods gave children life. Legal codes supported filial responsibilities with threats of harsh and swift punishment. Threats and promises exploited a sense of duty and unfulfilled desire for success in the younger generation.

In addition, the documents encouraged honor for the elderly in recognition of the need for continuity and the awe of mystery. Few adults survived the hardships of the ancient world to reach old age. White hair and old age retained their mystery with other generations as precious commodities. More than this, in Egypt aging adults represented the best avenue for grasping the wisdom of the ancestors. By learning from the past, the literature promised that a current generation could surpass other generations. An older generation was said to represent a gift from the gods through whom the next generation could learn to manage better their affairs and to carry out more efficiently the demands of daily responsibilities.

Unfortunately, even ancient oriental societies practiced respect and honor for the aging in an uneven manner. Laws tried to protect widows from the greed of their sons. Nevertheless, a rich elderly male in Egypt received more care than a poor one. Social disruption, urbanization, and the bureaucracies of monarchy certainly increased the uneven treatment of aging citizens. However, enfeebled elderly traditionally have experienced losses in aging. Yet the common ideals of ancient oriental societies cushioned those heartaches by bestowing upon the aging divine protection and affirmation of their worth. Thus, religion supported the rights and privileges of the enfeebled in their final years.

Extant literature of the ancient Near East preserved for subsequent generations a general appreciation of aging. Those values shared concerns similar to those reiterated in Israel's standards. This common theology remained for Israel and the Bible a central tenet for binding people together with each other and with God. Therefore the next chapter has been set aside to point out how this common theology impacted the faith and practice of Israel.

CHAPTER 3

God and the
Elderly in Israel

A Common Theology

Israel seems to have inherited for its faith and society many ancient oriental themes of respect for the older generation. The Hebrew Scriptures often describe attitudes and practices toward the elderly that reflect principles found in the literature of ancient Mesopotamia, Egypt, and Canaan. Such mutuality increases the difficulty of isolating unique biblical teachings on the issues of aging.

Universal acceptance of respect for the elderly does not decrease the value or truth of its principles. Instead, widespread appreciation for such attitudes and practices illustrates its importance. Indeed, respect for older citizens forms the skeleton on which early oriental societies were constructed. Unhealthy relationships between the generations bring social chaos. The Bible shares this concern and likewise seeks to strengthen social structures by relating respect for the elderly to faith in God.

LEGAL TRADITIONS, THE ELDERLY, AND SOCIAL STRUCTURES

As in ancient Mesopotamia, the Bible reinforces social structures through legislation supporting the authority of older members. Particular laws command children of all ages to treat the person and position of a parent as sacrosanct. Such statutes strengthen Israel's rings of power by establishing the leadership of the older generation. Likewise, eliminating abuse of aging parents encourages stability and support for people entering old age.

The literature of Israel often expresses outrage against verbal and physical abuse of vulnerable parents. Severe warnings and harsh penalties guard against filial neglect and disrespect. Statutes on this subject span Israel's legal collections.

Israel's traditional "Book of the Covenant" or "Covenant Code" (Exod. 20:22—23:33) classifies abuse of parents as a capital offense. Two particular statutes warn children who in some way attack the person of an enfeebled parent, or demean their parent's status. These parallel threats equate breaches of filial respect with those of physical violence. In succinct fashion the statutes warn:

> The one who strikes[1] father or mother shall be put to death.
> The one who curses[2] father or mother shall be put to death. (Exod. 21:15, 17)

Israel's laws tolerate no violation of the weakened condition of a parent. Both overt and covert abuse deserve the death penalty. Since a curse is the opposite of honor and respect and the source of neglect, it also represents an equally serious offense. Deuteronomy expresses a similar concern.

A set of twelve curses known as the Dodecalog (Deut. 27:15–26) follows a series of codes (Deuteronomy 12—26). The twelve curses are constructed as a liturgy. They include one against those who fail to honor parents. A cultic leader announces a curse and the people respond by saying "amen." The congregation's assent to the warning reminds all that respect for parents is tied directly to the relationship between God and the community. This treaty liturgy eliminates any excuse for neglecting family responsibilities.

> Cursed be the one who treats as despicable (dishonors) father or mother. (Deut. 27:16)[3]

According to this law a child who neglects filial responsibilities incurs the wrath of God.[4] Such a person treats parents as "accursed" or "without regard."

The so-called Holiness Code in Leviticus (Lev. [17] 18—26) reinforces the sacrosanct nature of parents by naming potential capital offenses (Lev. 20:1–27). These capital offenses state the consequences of offenses condemned in chapters 18—19. Leviticus 20:9–21 deals with sins in the family setting. Verse 9 not only begins the list; it elaborates on a common threat found in other law codes:

> For everyone who curses father or mother shall be put to death; the one
> cursing father or mother, let his/her blood be upon him/her. (Lev. 20:9)[5]

Again, cursing is the antithesis of "honoring" and so deserves the
death penalty. This passage expands earlier forms of this statute by
adding the phrase "his/her blood is upon him/her." The phrase justi-
fies further the death penalty.[6] It confirms that dishonoring a parent
deserves the death penalty.

A case of one such capital offense against parents is spelled out in
Deut. 21:18–21. In this instance parents are granted almost absolute
authority over a rebellious, maturing child. The passage recommends
that parents prosecute such a one and with the approval of community elders cut off this anarchy:

> A "stubborn" and "rebellious" child who will not listen to or obey the
> voice of either father or mother may be brought to the elders and
> declared a "glutton," and a "drunkard" and be stoned by the people of
> that city. (Deut. 21:18–21)[7]

In this instance the passage shows what it means for children to "take
lightly" their parents. Such children "curse" or "dishonor" them.
Community leaders, therefore, must purge this evil from their circles
to restore order and parental control. That goal is stated clearly in its
purpose clause: "All Israel will hear (of it) and be afraid." A threat of
execution protects the authority of the older generation and strengthens the rings of Israel's society.

However, in Israel's literature respect and honor of parents goes
beyond fear of their authority. That additional insight is illustrated
best by a text which by form and theological emphasis fits best with
the unique material of Israel. For that reason elements of it will be
discussed in more detail later. Nevertheless, it also reflects a shared
view of aging found outside of Israel. The passage from the Holiness
Code elaborates on respect for the signs of old age and equates
respect for these signs with fear of God:

> You shall rise up before the grayhead, and honor the face of an old
> person and you shall fear your God; I am the Lord. (Lev. 19:32)[8]

According to the shared views of old age, signs of aging, gray hair and
wrinkled skin, are to be honored. They are rare gifts given special
persons. The text uniquely calls on younger persons to honor the
signs of aging out of respect for God.

Summary

Israel's legal collections strengthen social structures and order by stressing obedience to and respect for the older generation. Such commands are reinforced by threats and religious obligations. Certainly God's special concern for the welfare of the elderly appears throughout various collections of law. These statutes reinforce universal motifs of a common theology of aging found in the ancient Orient.

PROPHETIC COMMUNITIES AND SUPPORT FOR SOCIAL STRUCTURES

Prophetic behavior in the literature of the Former Prophets also reflects a desire to reinforce the rings of authority in society. Though prophets critique various aspects of society, they do so to restore and protect order, not to devastate it. As messengers of God they hope to return righteousness and justice to social structures and to strengthen them against the deterioration of important religious values.

Recent studies in the phenomena of prophecy in Israel and the ancient Near East stress that prophetic messages often uphold official cults and societal structures, not oppose them.[9] Prophets enjoying prominent social status function within the worship centers of Israel and in direct support of the court. In these centers they advise the king, deliver oracles reinforcing the royal dynasty, and share duties common to those found elsewhere in the ancient Near East.[10]

Incidents recorded in Samuel-Kings mention the important role that many prophets assumed in supporting monarchy. Second Samuel 7 associates Nathan with the proclamation of an oracle establishing the dynasty of David's house (2 Sam. 7:11b). [11] The number and roles of court prophets seem to increase as monarchy expands until about four hundred prophets operate in Ahab's court (1 Kings 22:6).[12] Obviously they recognize in monarchy a type of order that could not be reproduced in a government by the judges (2 Sam. 7:10–11a).

Though many prophets do support the court, others prophesy outside of the political and social establishment. Because they oppose current policy such are forced out of the "social maintenance functions."[13] They begin separate communities or guilds operating as viable alternatives to the religious and social abuses of their monarchial society. Though not much is known about these communities, scholars assume that they reflect a pattern found in charismatic prophetic groups throughout the ancient Orient. Prophetic communities are mentioned in the Bible under the leadership of Samuel, later in the Northern Kingdom under the direction of Elijah, but even more so under Elisha (2 Kings 2—6).[14] Prophets living in alternative communities accept a strict social order and hierarchical control. They obey a master prophet who presides over them and instructs by example and word. They call their leader/teacher "father," and, in turn, disciples are termed "sons."[15] Elisha, for example, addresses Elijah as "father" (2 Kings 2:12) and later is called "father" himself by Joash, king of Israel: "My father, the horses and chariots of Israel" (2 Kings 13:14). A prophetic community, therefore, is organized around respect for the authority of one who normally is an older, more experienced prophet. The social structure of these peripheral prophetic communities resembles that of a family.[16]

A prophetic leader, unlike a parent or an elder, receives respect from disciples on the basis of unusual charismatic gifts. Elijah passes down his leadership by designating for Elisha a "double portion" inheritance of prophetic spirit (2 Kings 2:9–10). Neither age nor experience alone determines prophetic leadership, but a community "parent" may possess both. In prophetic circles even wisdom does not rival spiritual power as a sign of leadership. A prophetic "parent" performs miraculous deeds to take care of the needs of faithful followers (Samuel, Elijah, and Elisha), and at times shares with disciples the charismatic, ecstatic spirit (Moses, Samuel, and Elijah). Such a leader cares for the welfare of the prophetic community (2 Kings 4) and disciplines violators of its guidelines (e.g., Gehazi, 2 Kings 5:20–27).

Instead of proclaiming rebellion and anarchy, alienated prophetic communities generally demonstrate and reinforce social order based on traditional righteousness and justice. They set up their own rings of authority and offer them as an alternative. By example, the master prophet and disciples project a model of community based on mutual respect and commonality. In this way they attract both respect and scorn from those wedded to a society which through the influence of Baalism substitutes power and riches for values of respect and honor. Little wonder that Ahab considers Elijah a "troubler" (1 Kings 18:17) or "enemy" (1 Kings 21:20).

Outsider prophets reserve the right to reject kings and dynasties, to call for revolution, and to establish alternative communities. In no way, however, do peripheral prophets suggest that society depart from the common oriental goals of order and stability. Rather, their own community organization reinforces respect and honor for the "father" prophet. In this way alternative prophetic communities support Near Eastern traditions of respect for and submission to leadership of a parent-master. Thus they tighten the rings of hierarchical control in their community in order to critique the abuses of Israel's status quo. They support the common theology of respect for a leader-parent in the same way that society commonly honors its structures and leadership.

WISDOM LITERATURE, THE ELDERLY, AND SOCIAL STRUCTURES

Wisdom literature evidences a close relationship between its approach to aging and that of other ancient oriental societies. Its views deal with the essence of growing old as well as with familial relationships between the generations.[17] It reflects the views of the marketplace and the palace. The Book of Proverbs especially stresses how the roles of the elderly maintain a stable society.

Proverbs' emphasis on support for the older generation and their roles in society should not surprise a reader. Political and social viewpoints within the material often indicate an upper-class orientation for wisdom literature.[18] Though much of its imagery seems rural, it often addresses people who aspire to serve in aristocratic positions (e.g., Proverbs 25). It instructs the young to obey and deal wisely with rulers, elders, and skilled artisans that they might succeed in the organization (e.g., "The Sayings of the Wise" in Prov. 22:17—24:22 and proverbs in Prov. 16:10–15). Hence, it is perfectly natural that Israel's instructional material supports older, experienced instructors in particular and prominent social structures in general.

Respect for the Elderly as Educators

Wisdom literature throughout the ancient Near East enhances the roles of the elderly and designates them as sages and heirs of divine enlightenment. Egyptian and Israelite instruction both elevate the wisdom of professional teachers of the young.[19] By assuming that elderly should act as the teachers because of their experience, wisdom materials increase the value of older persons.

Since experience supposedly brought persons in touch with the secrets of life and success, wisdom literature instructs younger pupils to listen carefully to the words of the elders and to respect the insights of experience. Such cogent behavior insures success and wisdom for successive generations. Wisdom's call to respect parents and older persons roughly equals that of commanding a disciple to submit to the instruction of a famous teacher.

Individual proverbs rival legal traditions in demanding respect for parents. In this way wisdom teachers reinforce the authority and sense of worth of the older generation. They teach that anyone who disregards parents or teachers would face severe consequences:

> The person who curses father and mother, his/her lamp will be extinguished in thick darkness. (Prov. 20:20)

A person who takes lightly the teachings of parents would not survive difficult times. When the perils of deep darkness arrive, such fools would perish. In the above proverb, to take lightly the teachings of parents who can contribute so much seals the doom of any youth.

Proverbs subsequent to the sayings of Agur, son of Jakeh from Massa' (Prov. 30:1–4), reinforce the revered position of parental teachers.[20] A proverbial list of oppressive deeds and persons includes parental disrespect along with other behavioral problems:

> There are people who curse their fathers and do not bless their mothers. (Prov. 30:11)

Such actions rank with haughtiness, self-righteousness, and greediness as bad behavior (Prov. 30:12–14). Ultimately that type of person meets a horrible fate:

> The eye that mocks at father and despises obeying mother (scorns a mother's old age),[21] ravens of the valley will tear it out and vultures[22] will devour it. (Prov. 30:17)

This short collection of proverbs demonstrates a deep respect for parents and equates the scorning of a parent with other heinous crimes of society.

Respect for Elders as the Products of Wise Living

Israel also shares the assumption that one receives long life as a divine gift. Public opinion assumes gray or white hair comes as a benefit of some divine grant in return for righteous, wise living. Wisdom literature especially encourages this tenet. Proverbs teaches that religious and social discernment increases the number and quality of a disciple's days (Prov. 3:2, 16; 4:4, 10; 28:10). Rejecting the ways of wisdom provokes premature death (Prov. 10:16–17; 13:14; 14:27, 30; 19:16; 22:4).

Proverbs equates long life with following wisdom learned from experienced teachers. For example, a short proverb expresses the pragmatic side of the choice between life and death: "The law (instruction) of the wise is a fountain of life enabling one to elude the traps of death" (Prov. 13:14). Notice also how a crown of white hair comes as a sure sign of straight living and virtue: "White hair is a glorious crown; it is found in the way of righteousness" (Prov. 16:31). The religious axiom of these wisdom sayings also states clearly that wisdom for old age comes as a result of respect for God and its antithesis brings the opposite. "Fear of the Lord adds days; wickedness shortens the years" (Prov. 10:17).

Teachings from brief proverbs demonstrate that early in its history, Israel, like its neighbors, felt that old age came as a result of faithfulness to divine guidelines and adherence to wisdom tenets. White hair designates one who enjoys divine favor and indicates one who learned and obeyed the ways of virtue. In this way the short axioms reinforce a common aging theology of the ancient Near East.

Respect for Elders as Products of Piety

Lengthy instructional materials in Proverbs develop further the basic themes of this common theology. The genre found in Proverbs 1—9 reflects an entrenched view of older persons as teachers of the young. No doubt this perspective applies equally to official teachers in structured schools as well as to parents who informally teach children or grandchildren. Wisdom exhortations in this material thereby reinforce the authority of these instructors.

As in Egypt the basic role of the young learner is to listen and obey.

By doing this the younger generation insures success in life and can be spared the pitfalls of foolishness. For example, experienced teachers admonish students to pay attention to their helpful guidance.

> Listen, my son, take (to heart) what I am saying and you will multiply the years of your life. (Prov. 4:10)
>
> For they (my words) bring life to those who find them and health for all the body. (Prov. 4:22)

In these passages teachers reiterate anew that listening and obedience remain keys to multiplied years, life, and health.

Instructional materials further amplify wisdom's dependence on piety. Respect for God becomes a crucial factor for understanding life's complexities. Reliance on God rather than unaided intelligence lengthens life by helping one avoid misfortune. One passage illustrates this principle by expanding simpler expressions of wisdom's view of religious commitment:

> Fear of the Lord is the beginning of wisdom and knowledge of the Holy One is understanding.[23]
>
> For with me (wisdom) your days will be multiplied and years will be added to your life. (Prov. 9:10–11)[24]

Though this passage reflects a common assumption that respect for the deity brings long life, the instruction also reflects a developing theological consciousness that expresses Israel's unique contribution to wisdom material. In this passage the learner finds wisdom by respecting the Lord and moves into a relationship with the God of Israel in order to understand life. This divine understanding prolongs life.

The introduction to the Book of Proverbs reinforces how a listening child gains through following the instruction of parents. This statement provides the final context for stressing respect for and obedience to wise words.

> Listen, my child, to your father's instruction and do not forsake your mother's teaching for they are an adornment for your head and a necklace around your neck. (Prov. 1:8–9)

Proverbs' final chapter closes the book and its appendixes with excellent examples of listening children and wise parents. The unknown Lemuel, King of Massa' (Prov. 31:1–9), relates instruction that he received from his queen mother.[25] An acrostic poem in that chapter explains how a mature woman can be a successful, ambitious mother and wife. Such behavior again illustrates how the older generation possesses a diligence and capacity for great achievement. Little wonder that her children rise up to pronounce blessings on her and her husband sings her praises (Prov. 31:28). All enjoy many benefits from the gifted woman. Such anecdotes and poems also reinforce the common theology of the ancient Near East that recognizes the aging as capable guides to success and the wisdom of the ages. Such teachings reinforce their authority in the social structure and insure for them the adoration and support of younger generations.

CONCLUSION

Various types of Israel's literature reinforced societal stability through stressing respect for elders. Legal traditions equated parental abuse with capital offenses and cursed those who failed to respect their parents. These statutes likewise required respect and honor for the physical signs of old age. They left little doubt that God takes seriously the status and protection of the aging. Legal traditions thereby reinforced the rings of authority through which society achieved security and stability.

Prophetic communities by word and example also supported the stability of society. Some royal, cultic prophets strengthened the control of kingship through dynastic oracles and consultation. In this way they helped maintain the legitimacy of prominent social structures. Other prophets opposed the insensitivity of monarchy and its bureaucracy to issues of justice and religious purity and thereby made themselves unwelcome in royal cultic centers. Such outsiders organized alternative guilds or communities. These organizations reflected earlier concerns for respect and order but honored instead a charismatic leader. This type of community revered a prophet as its parent and demanded total obedience from its members. In different contexts both the maintenance and alternative prophetic communities supported the ideals of social stability and worked in different ways toward fulfilling its goals of order and respect so necessary for the welfare of the elderly.

Wisdom teaching stressed even more forcefully respect for members of the older generation. It promoted them as the ones who possess the secrets for successful living. For this reason, each succeeding generation insured its own success by learning the secrets of the elders and imitating their ways. That respectful response of younger learners needed to be expressed through listening and obedience. Respect for God further increased the imperative of obedience. In this sense, wisdom materials, like their legal and prophetic counterparts, reinforced the authority rings of society and respect for the older generation.

The social standing and welfare of Israel's older generation depended on support from a responsive and respectful societal structure. Frail elderly were especially vulnerable. To insure the future of traditional institutions, the Bible taught youth to submit to the authority of the older generation and to accept such as their teachers. It issued threats and appeals to self-interest to reinforce this basis for social stability. Such methods were used, however, to foster a climate that would encourage generational growth and interdependence.

Israel's traditional structures thereby became the framework through which God could act as the agent of blessing and deliverance for the elderly. When conflict and self-interest undermined the balance of respect and stability, they threatened also the work of God with the older generation. Hence, Israel's variations on the common theology of aging it inherited did not repudiate earlier ideals. Rather, Israel responded to conflict and defined more clearly its distinctive nature in light of its deity.

CHAPTER 4

Threats
to the Common
Theology of Aging

Ambiguity for the Elderly

The Bible portrays an Israel that not only shares the ideals of respect for the aging with its neighbors but also encounters similar struggles in practicing these values. A cursory reading of the materials indicates that relationships between the generations became strained in all periods of Israel's history. Though the Hebrew Bible does not record a history of treatment for the elderly, it contains indirect evidence that implies that in Israel practices toward the elderly often fell short of its ideals.

Hebrew Scriptures preserve a realistic picture of what it meant to age in Israel. Recorded anecdotes and stories present evidence that older generations occasionally felt the sting of negative attitudes and maltreatment. Even patriarchal families encountered intergenerational conflict. These struggles seem to intensify during the monarchy with its depersonalization of relationships. Biblical accounts indicate that older persons encountering negativism experienced confusion and ambiguity in the process.

Some biblical materials present images that could be interpreted as negative pictures of the aging process. These stereotypes record images of the elderly that could reinforce common misconceptions unless they are properly understood. Such types must be interpreted in a balanced fashion or they may foster generalizations about old age that do not take into account the full range of possibilities for the aging experience.

Chapter 4 begins with a study of passages that present aging stereotypes and then examines additional texts to enlarge an interpreter's perspective for understanding how passages fit into the experiences of aging. The discussion seeks to sensitize interpreters about aging realities in order to help them avoid a simplistic approach that unnecessarily increases anxiety about the aging process. Various passages do present types that when understood in isolation could reinforce misleading or negative images for old age. This discussion, however, encourages interpreters to better assess the data and to balance their discussion in light of a broad range of aging experiences.

AGING STEREOTYPES AND THE
AGING PROCESS

Misconceptions about aging tend to increase doubts about the ability of elder members to function productively in society. A stereotype that raises expectations to unrealistic levels or that seems defeatist and lowers the image of the elderly distorts the complex process of aging and handicaps the potential happiness of aging adults. An interpreter needs to understand the source of such distortions.

Stereotypes emerge partially out of the nature of storytelling. A story makes a specific point by incorporating one-dimensional characterizations which may distort what it means to age. Interpreters need to recognize biblical one-dimensional pictures of aging adults and balance these with additional examples. Otherwise, flat images or types[1] may lead to generalizations that would undermine the morale and respect of the elderly. This section of the chapter mentions some one-dimensional characterizations of aging persons. Sensitivity to this aspect of narrative poetics aids interpreters in balancing biblical negative and glorified images of the elderly.

Elderly Become Physically Disabled

On the surface the Bible seems to present old age as the loss of health and the stage of severe infirmities. Biblical characters often experience aging as a mixed blessing. In these instances the Bible agrees with a common aging philosophy which understands it as a period of physical degeneration. In such cases God's blessing seems remote in its infirmities.

The Hebrew Scriptures do list a number of less than healthy and well-adjusted aging heroes. Abraham and Sarah suffer depression in their old age as they grieve over having no son and being past the normal age of having children (Genesis 15—18). Isaac and Jacob become blind in their old age (Gen. 27:1–2; 48:10). Isaac trembles when angry as if suffering some neurological disability (Gen. 27:33). Eli, the priest in Shiloh during the early years of Samuel, becomes blind and overweight. Due to his shock upon hearing about the deaths of his sons and especially the capture of the ark of the covenant, he falls off his seat and dies of a broken neck (1 Sam. 4:12–18). A narrator blames this accident on his old age and overweight condition (1 Sam. 4:18).

The Bible portrays certain parts of old age as less than pleasant for a number of early heroes. Eli and Samuel endure bitter disappointment when their sons become dishonest and unfit to continue their rule (1 Sam. 2:12–17, 22–25; 8:1–5). David grieves over the outcome of his weak and ineffective actions as a father (2 Samuel 11—1 Kings 2:11). His sons and his kingdom rebel against him in a struggle for the throne. Solomon, by the closing days of his reign, apparently loses his religious moorings and his father's empire (1 Kings 11).

Passages also describe elderly who become feeble and easy to manipulate, as in the cases of Isaac (Genesis 27) and David (1 Kings 1). Noah and Lot act foolishly when they get drunk (Genesis 9, 19). Losses embitter Naomi (Ruth 1:20–21). Death and filial dishonesty strip Jacob of family and leave him exposed, grieving, and vulnerable (Gen. 37:34–35). The context of Numbers 20 implies that Moses sinned horribly while grieving after the death of his sister Miriam (Num. 20:1–12). All of these examples seem to support the stereotype that old age is a time of physical degeneration and disability.

On the other hand, the Bible also glorifies certain of its heroes by describing them as models of good health and vigor in their old age. Moses is said to be the ideal physical specimen as an aged leader. Upon his death a tribute is recorded saying: "His eye was not dim nor was his natural force (fertility) lessened" (Deut. 34:7). Later, Caleb brags about his excellent health when he says: "I am as strong today (age eighty-five) as in the day when Moses sent me; as my strength was then, so my strength is now, forever and for going out and coming in" (Josh. 14:10b–11). However, note that he conquers the fortress of Kiriath-sepher by offering his daughter Achsah as a bride to the one who led the battle, rather than assaulting it himself. In these passages,

Israel memorializes both Moses and Caleb for having excellent health in their old age.

Though biblical narratives often type the elderly as enfeebled and sometimes disabled, it must be clear from other passages that a wider range of possibilities does exist for the aging. No generalization about the aging experience should be drawn from either the negative images or the glorified health of clan heroes. Rather, one can recognize that while some abilities may decline with old age, the degeneration of health with its resulting disabilities may not occur in all elders.[2] Healthy aging adults mentioned in biblical narratives remain substantially self-sufficient, happy, and productive.

Elderly Become Intransigent

Respect for aging adults at times declines because they suffer under the image of intransigent conservatism and skepticism. Unfortunately, certain events prominently underline this behavior of some aging adults and its potential harm. For example, an older prophet brings about the death of a younger one because of his skepticism (1 Kings 13:1–32). The younger prophet journeys from Judah to Bethel to denounce the golden calf of Jeroboam. He also vows not to eat or drink during that mission. The older prophet lures him to his home to enjoy forbidden hospitality by lying in pious words:

> I also am a prophet as you and an angel spoke to me by the word of the Lord, saying, "Bring him back with you to your house, that he may eat bread and drink water." But he lied to him. (1 Kings 13:18)

The skeptical prophet manipulates the tentative respect of his younger colleague and costs the younger prophet his life. Through what the narrator calls a lie he grants the young man permission to break his promise and the results are fatal. A lion later is said to kill the young man on the way home. Only then does the older prophet realize the young man had spoken the truth. Unfortunately, it is too late. This story honestly relates a disbelieving attitude which elders sometimes display.

Other passages represent the aging as a type who idealizes the past and depreciates the present. After the exile elderly worshipers undermine the rejoicing over the rebuilding of the temple. With great sentimentality, older persons weep as the foundations of the second temple are laid. They remember the temple of Solomon and realize how glorious the lost structure had been. The new temple foundation seems insufficient when compared with the earlier magnificence that Babylon destroyed (Ezra 3:12–13). Haggai may be addressing a similar pessimism in his words to those who constructed the second temple (Hag. 2:3).[3] Then as now certain elderly tend to glorify past accomplishments and to devalue the present and thereby undermine their leadership role.

On the contrary, not every aging adult in the Bible is skeptical and intransigent (e.g., Moses, Joshua, and Caleb). The advantage of having older advisers who are experienced and wise (Ahithophel, 2 Sam. 15:31, 34; 16:20–23; 17:23; the elders of Solomon, 1 Kings 12:6–8) balances this negative type. Though some aging adults value earlier events more than the present, others as elder leaders retain a flexible vision for the future and deal skillfully with the present. The stereotype of intransigent older citizens must be understood as a warning against such behavior, not as a characterization of old age.

Elderly Become Unable to Enjoy Sexual Experiences

Birth announcement narratives occasionally center on the difficulty of conceiving in old age (2 Kings 4:14–17; Luke 1:7, 18). Some of this concern relates to the physical changes that come for a woman after menopause but, indirectly, some of the narratives reinforce common misunderstandings about the sexual abilities and interests of older adults. Parts of the dialogue imply that elderly men and women cannot perform satisfactorily in intercourse.[4] Indirectly, the Bible reflects and refutes these ideas.

The main point of the Isaac birth announcements in Genesis (15—21) seems to be the impossibility of his birth. God alone provides the "laughter" (Isaac) desired by Abraham and Sarah. This narrative also includes secondary comments about old age emphasizing that Isaac's birth would be an improbable event. The dialogue reflects somewhat the common stereotype that neither aging men nor women can perform sexually very well.

In response to one birth announcement, Abraham laughs at how preposterous it would be that Sarah and he could produce a child in their old age (Gen. 17:17).[5] When a messenger tells Sarah that she would give birth to a son, she also laughs (Gen. 18:12). Her nervous laughter shows her despair. A narrator elaborates on the hopelessness of the situation by noting that she had passed the time of menopause and having a child in her "extreme old age" lay beyond the realm of possibility. Finally, Sarah expresses how she truly feels when she says:

> After I have become this old will I enjoy sex enough (that I would get pregnant) since my husband (*'adonai*) is an old man? (Gen. 18:12)

Sarah assumes that neither she nor her husband could perform well enough to conceive a child. She appears to worry about their sexual dysfunction in old age. Obviously, God overrides all of their problems and fears. Within nine months Sarah gives birth to Isaac (laughter). Nothing remains too hard for the Lord (Gen. 18:14).

The Bible also dismisses this stereotype about aging in the birth narratives of Moab and Ben-ammi (Gen. 19:33–38). Traditions about Lot mention old age and the fears of his two daughters (Gen. 19:31–32). He is too old to find them a husband. However, he remains strong enough that even while intoxicated he could inseminate his daughters and provide sons for them (Gen. 19:33–36). Both birth narratives glorify their respective patriarchs and establish national genealogies. Secondarily, they demonstrate that healthy aging adults need not fear loss of their sexual prowess or interests in old age.

David, the warrior king, generally obliterates the sexual stereotype of the aging process. The succession narrative shows him to be a poor father with his children, but most passages describe his success as a lover (2 Sam. 6:22; 11:3–5). Only when near his death does he seem to fit the stereotype. To "warm" the ailing king officials place a beautiful maiden, Abishag, in his bed.[6] When David does not "warm" to this beauty, officials surmise that death is near. With this they know that he lacks the strength to provide for the well-being of the kingdom (1 Kings 1:1–4). This example, however, does not indicate what healthy elders can do; rather, it shows how a severe terminal illness can cause sexual dysfunction.

To the contrary, other anecdotes about Bible heroes indicate that healthy aging persons can experience mutually enjoyable relationships in sex. God's blessings assume growth in this area also. Certainly, declining physical strength does not rule out a wide range of possibilities concerning the abilities of an aging body.

Elderly Become Senile

Aging adults who worry about their future mental health can also receive comfort from the Hebrew Scriptures. On the surface the Bible seems to support the senility stereotype. It mentions a number of older persons who experience declining health, increasing dependence, and marked differences in behavior. On the other hand, other incidents involving older persons indicate that old age does not necessarily lead to helplessness or a brain disease such as senile dementia or Alzheimer's disease.[7] Even where one might be handicapped by a physical problem such as blindness, the mind can remain clear.

A narrative about an aging Jacob represents a good biblical case study of a strong-minded but feeble elder. Though tribal concerns dominate the text, some insights about aging can be gained secondarily. Jacob is dying and suffering under blindness when he blesses his grandsons, in particular the sons of Joseph. He reverses their order of importance when he places his hands on their heads, setting his left hand on Manasseh, the firstborn, and his right one on Ephraim, the youngest. When Joseph angrily tries to move his hands to the proper sons, Jacob refuses to change, saying: "I know, my son, I know" (Gen. 48:19). He is perfectly aware of what he is doing and resists being pampered or forced to change his actions despite his illness and impending death. In the passage his mind functions with clarity. Thereby the story gives his unorthodox decision credit for Ephraim's rise to supremacy.

In general, narratives in Genesis show positive expectations for aging parents as they portray them as heads of the clan and advisers for the children. They deliver blessings that determine inheritance rights and future status. Elderly Abraham secures a wife for Isaac by sending a servant bonded to him by an oath (Genesis 24).[8] Blind, aging Isaac in turn blesses Jacob with such finality that no one could counteract or adjust it. Even after aging parents turn over most of their work to children, their offspring continue to seek and cherish their advice.

Other materials also describe the elderly as the counselors and inspiration for the second generation. In Exodus Jethro, the father-in-law of Moses, rescues an already mature leader, Moses, by helping him reorganize his administration of justice in the wilderness (Exodus

18). Joshua (Josh. 13:1; 23:1–2) and Caleb (Josh. 15:13–19; Judg. 1:11–15), survivors of an older generation, inspire parts of the conquest settlement of Canaan.

A lesser-known aged hero in the throne succession narrative (2 Samuel 9—20, 1 Kings 1—2) also demonstrates the attitudes of good mental health. This wealthy elder statesman (eighty years old), Barzillai, the Gileadite from Rogelion, supports David during Absalom's rebellion. He along with others sustains the king and his forces while his defeated, weary army recovers in Mahanaim (2 Sam. 17:27–29; 19:31–39). These provisions seem to have helped turn the crisis in David's favor. Out of gratitude to Barzillai's loyalty David asks him to become a part of his court. The story points out why Barzillai rejected David's offer to move to Jerusalem, explaining in the following manner:

> How long have I yet to live that I should go up with the king of Jerusalem? I am now eighty years old. Can I distinguish between good and bad? Or can your servant taste what I eat or what I drink?
>
> Or can I hear any more the voice of singing men or women? Why then should your servant be an added burden to my lord and king? . . .
>
> Please let your servant return that I might die in my own city near the grave of my father and my mother. (2 Sam. 19:34–37a)

Gently and perceptively Barzillai refuses David's generosity. He reminds David that his aging infirmities would keep him from enjoying life at the court for he suffers from taste and hearing maladies common to old age. In this sense the narrative balances both positive and negative aspects of aging. Like Jacob, Barzillai demonstrates clear thinking and an independent spirit and yet still suffers some effects of growing older. In place of himself Barzillai suggests that David promote one of his own, Chimham (a son?), to prominence in the court. The king kisses and blesses Barzillai and returns to Jerusalem leaving him in a friendly environment where he could face death with meaning.

Examples of elderly leaders recorded in the Hebrew Scriptures indicate that living to a ripe, old age does not necessarily mean that one becomes useless and senile. Dementia is a disease that healthy postmature adults generally avoid.[9] Most aging adults need not fear its terrible consequences.

Summary: Interpreting Aging Stereotypes

Though biblical types produce some impressions about aging that are helpful, they do not provide a complete description of old age. Their impressions require additional evidence to broaden the range of possibilities for the aging process. Biblical interpreters need to balance the positive images of glorified, aging ancestors with those of bitter, declining, and dependent elders. This methodology defines aging in its broader range of experiences and avoids simplistic generalizations about old age.

MONARCHY AND DECLINING LEADERSHIP OF THE ELDERLY

The literature of Israel generally portrays older people in a favorable light despite an occasional typing of the aging experience. However, these traditions also allude to a process of restructuring society under the rise of monarchy. Its modifications would reorganize Israel's society in a way that conflicted with earlier, more equitable traditions and leadership.[10] At the center of Israel's resistance to bureaucratization stand Israel's natural leaders, the "elders."[11] Such traditional leadership includes prominent citizens, landowners, family or clan leaders, and high ranking warriors.[12]

Triumph of Monarchy Over Leadership of Elders

Israel's traditional leadership during the period of Judges seems based on both "charismatic designation" and the clan position each already holds. Leadership during this period evidences a set of values and methods quite different from those of state power and bureaucracies.[13] In this period local leaders who seek wealth and influence in the manner of kings (Gideon and Abimelech) meet fierce resistance.

Biblical laws and stories often encourage a simpler, egalitarian style of leadership. Such texts ascribe to socioeconomic values that teach mutual aid and cooperation. Land is owned by extended families and must never be sold for profit. Aid for the vulnerable must always be extended and no interest can be charged on loans. They value justice performed in an even and compassionate manner. Even Israel's view of God generally reflects these principles.

Military pressure from the Philistines (1150–1050 B.C.E.) seems to have doomed the intertribal movement and its leaders. That external pressure together with internal disarray and corruption can be said to have moved Israel closer to the entrenchment of monarchy and its socioeconomic system. A monarchial system secures its prosperity and continuity through a monopoly of leadership by powerful families and priesthoods. The dynastic and bureaucratic tendencies of monarchy eventually overwhelmed Israel's natural leadership and their leveling influence.

Israel's literature contains numerous examples of how the triumph of monarchy affected the leadership of elders. Passages in 1 Kings show how a bureaucracy developed in Jerusalem which eventually excluded elders from national leadership. Though David laid the basis for this system with his conquest of Jerusalem and his census (2 Samuel 24), the institutions of monarchy seem to have reached their zenith during the reign of Solomon.

Solomon's division of Israel (northern tribes) into twelve districts and the appointment of chronies and relatives as officers over these districts may be one instance of Solomon's undermining of the leadership of clan elders (1 Kings 4:1–21). His system of forced labor and the heavy burden of taxes represent other examples of the triumph of monarchy and the professional technicians and political appointees that it spawned (1 Kings 4:22–28; 5:13–18; 9:15–28). Under the rule of Solomon, the "elders of Israel" function as ceremonial leaders (1 Kings 8:1–4) rather than as wielders of political power.

The influence of traditional values and leadership on state policy declines even more after the death of Solomon. Rehoboam totally rejects the humane concerns of Solomon's advisers. His older advisers reflect an allegiance to traditional socioeconomic values. These older leaders argue for a "lightening of the yoke on the people." Younger advisers *(yeladim)*, contemporaries of Rehoboam, relish only the goals of monarchy—increased power through harsher treatment and heavier taxes (1 Kings 12:10–15). Rehoboam accepts the advice of the younger generation and ruptures the kingdom. Elders in the north lead a rebellion against the monarchial values of Rehoboam and his bureaucracy and establish their own kingdom under Jeroboam.

The Hebrew Scriptures chart how eventually the socioeconomic power of monarchy triumphed over elder leadership in the Northern

Kingdom. By the reign of Ahab, elders seem powerless to affect public policy. Elders generally support Ahab's designs for war (1 Kings 20:7–8). They are docile and dominated enough to allow Jezebel to utilize them to strip Naboth of his vineyard and life (1 Kings 21:11). They now abuse the value system that they formerly espoused. Even the elders of Judah unite with royal officials in oppressing the people (Isa. 3:14) and in idolatrous worship (Ezek. 8:11–12).

The Bible mentions how the triumph of monarchy in both kingdoms effectively eliminates the leadership of elders in national affairs and therefore the influence of their leveling values. Royal administrators control the government and thereby relegate older, traditional leaders to local, judicial positions in agricultural communities and villages (Deuteronomy 21).[14] From the time of Ahab to the end of kingship, royal interests in both kingdoms dominate the more responsive leadership of the elders.

Leadership of Elders After the Monarchy

Only with the exile and the dissolution of the monarchy does eldership regain its national influence. In a letter from Jeremiah to the exiles in Babylon he addresses elders as leaders (Jer. 29:1–2). Likewise, the "Elders of Israel" approach Ezekiel to inquire of the Lord (Ezek. 20:1ff). Once again in exile, stripped of a king, elders return to preeminence and again represent the needs of the people (Ezek. 8:1; 14:1).

After the exile, elders join with the local governor to rebuild the temple (Ezra 5:5; 6:6–7). Elders receive credit for successfully completing the project under the inspiration of Haggai and Zechariah (Ezra 10:8) and once again represent all Israel as important national leaders.

Leadership of Elders During the Hellenistic Period

Elders in Israel exercise leadership primarily in community political affairs during the periods of Greek rule (330–150 B.C.E.). Domination of the country by Alexander of Macedon and the Ptolomy and Seleucid dynasties seems to have increased the political dependence of the people upon family or clan heads.

The Book of Judith tells a story describing a community organization that utilizes elders as leaders.[15] They hear complaints and judge at the gate. Judith performs her courageous feat because other community leaders could not withstand the power of Holofornes.

In the accounts of the Maccabean revolt (3 and 4 Maccabees), elders play significant roles as advisers. They represent wisdom and restraint. Old men talk young warriors out of fighting. Elders try to influence royal decisions. Unfortunately, kings fall victim to their pride and again reject seasoned advice and impulsively act as the following quote indicates: "He had grown bold and dismissed all restraints."[16] Even though royalty continues to frustrate the advice of elders, such still act as wise counselors.

The materials of Maccabees condemn the brutality of Greeks as they persecute Jews by cruelly forcing old men, covered with gray hair, stiff and stooped with age, to go on a forced march at a rapid pace.[17] The horror accounts express over this action demonstrates the high respect that society held for older citizens. For them elderly persons represent the gentle spirit of peace and wisdom of the ages. The people's dependence on such leadership becomes clear in other recorded examples.

To demonstrate that religious reason is stronger than emotions, 4 Maccabees tells of the suffering of some righteous martyrs.[18] Though the historicity of these stories may be questioned, they contain several examples of attitudes toward the elderly. These incidents do not teach the ideals of respect for the elderly as much as they glorify members of that age group who place religious convictions over life itself.

The stories describe a number of courageous elderly Jews. When Eleazer, an aged priest, comes before Antiochus, the Greek king addresses him with unusual respect. The words may be spoken in jest to beguile Eleazer to violate his conscience and to eat swine's flesh. White hair seems to move the king to grant mercy if Eleazer would eat unclean food. When the old man refuses and therefore is tortured violently, the king's courtiers, seemingly in pity over his old age, plead with him to pretend to taste the flesh. He replies: "I will not be a model of impiety to the young."[19] Such a passage not only indicates a universal respect for the aged, it also indicates that elderly possess the resources to sacrifice themselves in excruciating pain for their faith. In order to fulfill a leadership responsibility an older person can endure anything. Through religious reason the aging can enjoy renewed strength in spirit. As the obituary states:

> Oh, blessed old age, white head, revered, life loyal to the law, and consummated by the faithful seal of death.[20]

That same courage is also found in an elderly mother who sees her seven sons tortured to death. Maccabees eulogizes her as the "greatest hero," the "mother of a nation." Her sons endure horror and death for the Torah at her urging. When her tormentors try to seize her, she throws herself into the fire that none might touch her body.[21] She, as Eleazer, demonstrates that despite age and pain, raw courage comes when religious reason is sovereign over emotions. Elders thereby are challenged to act as the inspiration for a younger generation in the battle for the Torah against the forces of uncleanness.

Summary

Israel's dependence on the leadership of elders varied considerably during its history. Its early clan-centered society granted general credence to the opinions of its elders. Such leadership later represented the leveling ideals of clan unity, aid for the vulnerable, and mutual interdependence. Later, however, monarchy monopolized Israel's leadership with its consolidated power and bureaucracy. Its favoritism encouraged the manipulation of power and wealth, which vastly limited and undermined the leadership of Israel's traditional leaders. Some elders even joined with the bureaucracy to perpetuate the consolidation of wealth and control. Eldership itself was confined to local judicial positions.

The fall of monarchy brought about a restoration of the influence of elders. They led the exilic community in Babylon and the postexilic restoration of the nation. Persecution under Antiochus Epiphanes and its resulting religious crisis forced the people to depend even more on their guidance and moral examples. In each period, however, the leadership of elders varied with shifts in society.

Israel's experiences teach how a society may diminish the role of its concerned leaders and terminate hope for a system based on justice and righteousness. They also show that at times aging leadership fails to honor the roles of teaching and practicing fear of God, truthfulness, and honesty (Exod. 18:21), and thereby incurs the wrath of a just God. The declining influence of Israel's natural traditional leaders may explain to some degree how Israel's political institutions during the monarchy lost touch with the liberating God of the exodus and the equitable heritage through which God's blessings and deliverance operate.

POSTEXILIC PESSIMISM, DEATH, AND AGING

Exile in Babylon and a humble restoration in Israel seems to have crushed the nation's optimistic spirit. Wisdom at that point begins to struggle in a new way with realities as dark as those that greeted Egypt's loss of its Early Kingdom. A spirit of pessimism threatens proverbial, glowing descriptions of the blessings of old age. Though little is known about this postexilic community, it can be said that powerlessness increased its awareness of the handicaps and limitations of life itself and old age in particular. God's blessings seem very remote.

Ecclesiastes examines the roots of the dark experiences of life. Qoheleth, apparently an aging teacher, questions the values of life that diminish under the specter of death. The teacher knows by experience that youth, not old age, possesses blessings and opportunities. Age and experience reap handicaps and hardships for which wisdom has no answer. Old age limits the options of life and makes it tenuous:

> Better a poor but wise youth than an old but foolish king who no longer has the sense to heed warnings. For the former can emerge from a dungeon to become king; while the latter, even if born to kingship, can become a pauper. (Eccles. 4:13–14)

Unfortunately, as Ecclesiastes points out, foolishness carries a greater liability for the elderly than for the young. Success easily slips away from the aging. Darkness clouds the horizons of the elderly because death approaches as an immediate enemy. This ultimate enigma of Qoheleth crushes all remaining potential for successful human endeavors and achievements.

In a moving poem, the teacher pictures death as a thunderstorm that eventually shatters the house or body in which a person lives:[22]

So remember appreciatively your Creator (vigor) in the days of your youth, before those days of hardship come and those years arrive in which you will say: "I have no pleasure in them"; before sun and light and moon and stars grow dark, and the clouds come back again after the rain. (Eccles. 12:1–2)

Thus old age creates all the more an awareness that death is arriving. Elders more than any other age group begin to deal directly with death. In this process an aging Qoheleth recognizes that young persons should enjoy daily the precious gift of youth before its strength ebbs away.

Associating death with old age as does Ecclesiastes affords a mixed blessing for all elderly. Many face a slow death in old age. The analogy is inevitable and its stigma weighs heavily as a burden. On the other hand, when an older generation learns like Qoheleth to move with sensitivity and openness toward death, aware of its consequences, it offers hope to fearful younger pilgrims. Aging adults can teach the next generations to live each precious day with vigor and gratitude.

Living in the shadow of death allows the teacher, Qoheleth, to describe the death process vividly as the degeneration of a weakening body:

> In the day when the keepers of the house tremble,
> And the strong men are bent,
> And the maids that grind cease, grown few,
> And the ladies that peer through the windows grow dim,
> And the doors to the street are closed
> When the noise of the grinding is low;
> And one wakes up with the singing of a bird,
> And the sounds (daughters) of music are dying down,
> When one feels afraid of heights
> And there is terror on the way
> Though the almond tree may flourish
>   The locust shall fail
> And the caperberry bush may bud again;
> Because a person sets out for an eternal house,
> With mourners going around in the street—
> Before the silver cord is loosened (snaps)
> and the golden bowl is shattered,
> The pitcher is broken at the spring,
> and the wheel breaks at the cistern
> Then the dust returns to the earth,

As it was,
and the lifebreath returns to God
Who gave it.[23]

(Eccles. 12:3-8)

As perceptive elderly view death directly and openly anticipate its inevitability, they view life's values in a radically different way. The experiences of Qoheleth prove how fragile success can be and how much more crucial should be intimate relationships. In this light wisdom at best appears to be tentative and work settles into an opportunity to do good. Though many aging feel burdened by the specter and grief of death, they may offer humanity its finest lesson by helping all rearrange their priorities in light of this ominous teaching aid.

The Hebrew Scriptures make very clear that old age by its nature presents the aging with uneasy alternatives. However, the physical and psychological burdens of aging need not defeat the elderly. Rather, each may accept the challenges of an aging body and still teach others to value time, health, and relationships as the teacher stresses.

CONCLUSION

No theology is integrated easily into practice. Israel also struggled with her neighbors against similar temptations of intergenerational conflict, misleading stereotypes, and political intrigue. At times the nation resembled pilgrims in search of their value system and subject to pessimism and despair. However, as the next chapter will indicate, the outcome of Israel's views was never in doubt.

In spite of social struggles and resulting ambiguity, the values of dignity and respect for aging creations of God survived in Israel. Instead of negating the worth of the elderly, even strained intergenerational relationships reaffirmed positive expectations for persons who age. Their leadership role, while changing, remained intact. In facing the ambiguity of death, their leveling values survived the impact of monarchy and foreign domination. They reestablished themselves as the teachers of divine wisdom for the young. Israel's common struggles to retain respect for the aging eventually led it to a recognition of the contributions of the elderly to its theology and value systems.

CHAPTER 5

Israel's Variations on the Common Theology

A brief survey of what has been called Israel's common theology on treatment of the elderly indicates that several unique emphases are interspersed within statements that undergird social structures. Such texts contain certain dimensions that go beyond legitimating the rule of the powerful. These insights reflect important characteristics of Israel's faith. Their distinctive flavor emerges from Israel's experiences with God and responds to violations of its traditional values. Interpreters may isolate at least three such emphases woven within texts studied in previous chapters.

First of all, biblical texts expressing a common concern for the elderly do so with a fervor surpassing that found in other literatures. A comparison between penalties threatened by laws clearly shows this tendency. In Mesopotamia physical abuse of one's father might cost one's hand; verbal abuse might lead to disgrace, slavery, or loss of inheritance. Israel's laws consider either form of parental abuse as a capital offense. They rank striking, cursing, mocking, and neglecting a parent equally with murder and other heinous crimes. Such crimes demand the ultimate punishment. Israel's legislation on parental welfare expresses a passion unequaled in other common theologies.

Second, biblical laws and teachings evenly support both father and mother. Mesopotamian laws support both parents, but not to the degree of equity found in Israel's traditions. In Mesopotamia a statute against hitting one's father does not mention the mother. On the other hand, an offense against a mother in Israel warrants as severe a punishment as one against a father. Wisdom literature encourages younger learners to listen carefully to the insights of their mother. Her views may aid a member of the younger generation as much as those of a father. Either parent, even when weakened by loss of physical and economic power, merits equal respect in the Bible. In materials more directly tied to the theology of Israel that appears even clearer.

In the third place, Israel's laws relate common intergenerational matters to Israel's relationship with God even more than the laws of Egypt and Mesopotamia. Biblical passages equate support for the rings of Israel's society with loyalty to the God of Israel and concern for a separated religious community. The Holiness Code directly suggests that respect for the elderly arises out of concerns rooted in the nature of God. Wisdom literature in its more theological instruction associates fear of God with listening to parental teaching. These theological and religious concerns especially dominate Israelite variations on these teachings.

Israel's unique emphases woven within expressions of respect for the elderly demonstrate the perspectives around which the Bible structures its variations on the subject. The intensity of Israel's concerns for the welfare of aging parents indicates a traditional orientation toward justice. Suggestions for an evenhanded treatment of parents certainly reflect the ideals of a God who saved the powerless from Egypt. Israel's stress of loyalty to God and parents certainly reflects a central axiom for faith and a perceived basis for divine blessings or curses. Therefore, with these distinctive emphases in mind, it is important to study Israel's variations on the common theology of the ancient Orient.

CARE FOR THE ELDERLY AND THE
GOD OF JUSTICE

Protection for the aging in Israel issues out of the center of God's nature as much as out of a desire to support the structures of society. Though other gods like those in Egypt support *ma'at* or justice, none does so with the intensity of the God of Israel. Divine compassion demands concern for the weak and disenfranchised.

Traditional values and their adherents urge support for the poor, handicapped, widow, orphan, and stranger.[1] Such warn that faithfulness on this matter determines the future of any contractual relationship between the people and their God. The God of the exodus and giver of the land does not tolerate neglect of vulnerable persons. Curses flow on those who ignore such concerns. Blessings encourage those who faithfully keep them.

At the heart of Israel's understanding of the justice of God rests the exodus memory. Here the God of the ancestors identifies with an oppressed group of slaves against the power cult of Egypt. The groaning of an afflicted people and their cries for help motivate their God to see, hear, and remember them (Exod. 2:23–25; 3:7–10; 6:6–7). Through signs and wonders God redeems and delivers the lowly victims of Egypt's cruelty and brings them to a land of promise. Through this experience God reveals an intense passion for the welfare of strangers and the dispossessed. Little wonder that justice themes remain such an important part of the messages of the law and prophets.

Justice themes in the law reinforce care for the elderly who without some additional support might enter a new stage of poverty. Laws in the Book of the Covenant stress the intensity of God's concern for such persons (Exod. 22:22–26; 23:9–11). The Holiness Code expresses its standards in even stronger terms. Often laws prescribe direct ways to provide for the poor and hungry (Lev. 19:9–13). Since old age may bring physical disability, protection for frail elderly may hinge on obedience to guidelines for treatment of the handicapped. Note the following concerns about abuse of the blind and deaf:

> You shall not curse the deaf or before the blind put something that might cause them to stumble. Rather you must fear your God: I am the Lord. (Lev. 19:14)

Elderly often suffer impairment of hearing or sight. This commandment is particularly relevant for their handicaps.

Leviticus forbids the harming or ridiculing of a handicapped person. No one is allowed to speak a curse against a deaf person. Deafness renders a person defenseless against words. The statute likewise condemns placing an obstacle in the path of one who cannot see well enough to avoid it. Hearing and sighted persons who hurt or ridicule such helpless ones arouse the anger of the God of Israel. Certainly this inconsiderate behavior would never be done by a person who fears the God of justice. God by nature intensely defends the defenseless. Respect for Israel's God and standards provides the only real antidote for carelessness or cruelty against the handicapped.

Respect for the God of justice therefore motivates respect for an older person. The Holiness Code characteristically reinforces such statutes with a formulaic self-revelation of Israel's God: "I am the Lord."[2] For example, it has already been noted how such a refrain reinforces the honoring of the elderly:

> You shall rise up before the white head, and honor the face of an old man, and you will fear your God. I am the Lord. (Lev. 19:32)

Liturgical rhetoric in this passage identifies respect for the characteristics of aging with feelings of divine dread. Fear of the divine includes worship of, respect for, and a sense of awe at who God represents. God by nature requires younger worshipers to honor certain physical signs of aging for these designate special persons, honored and protected by an awesome God.

Early proverbial passages also express intense concern against exploitation of elderly parents. Though such proverbs reflect commonly shared viewpoints, note the outrage in the following statements:

> A person who robs father and mother and says, "There is nothing wrong with it," becomes the accomplice of a murderer. (Prov. 28:24)

This proverb addresses the behavior of a child who has the power to victimize parents. The passage equates this abhorrent, unnatural crime with murder. In the text children embezzle money that parents need for future support with a calloused attitude admitting neither shame nor guilt. The plundering of aging parents may become an actual act of murder when destitute parents depend on limited resources for survival. It is easy to understand why the proverb places an uncaring child in the same category with murderers.

> A child who wrongly treats his/her father and evicts his/her mother becomes a source of shame and disgrace. (Prov. 19:26)

With evenhandedness the proverb warns those who would wrongly treat an aging parent. The saying especially addresses the unique problem of widowhood. As already noted, widows lack power and frequently are victims of injustice. Strong-willed sons possess the power to evict the widow when she loses the protection of her husband. This text uses strong language to heap shame upon an adult child guilty of mistreatment of a vulnerable parent. Such a person is *ben mevish umahpir* (son of shame and reproach). Instead, a child should properly care for a parent when that one enters a more dependent season of life.

Themes in the above proverbs find their equivalents in literatures from other ancient nations. However, the intensity of outrage at such injustice sets apart Israel's faith. These proverbs reflect Israel's concerns for the poor, weak, and widow as characterized in exodus theology. As in the legal materials so in Proverbs God fights for the poor (Prov. 22:22–23). With this same passion God condemns mistreatment of parents and supports their deliverance.

CARE FOR THE ELDERLY AND HONORING PARENTS

Justice for the elderly in the ancient Orient essentially depends on satisfactory relationships between children and parents. Consequently, the Bible and parallel literatures concentrate on reinforcing the responsibilities of the parent-child relationship. In Israel, respect for parents moves beyond fearing harsh punishment in cases of parental abuse. One positive formulation of this respect appears in the series known as the Ten Commandments or Decalogue. In the context of Exodus 20 the command becomes an integral part of Israel's Sinai declaration of loyalty to God. In this code its form differs from negative apodictic laws. A formal analysis of it in various codes provides a longitudinal study of an important key to Israel's support of the elderly.

Number five in the list of "ten words," it reads simply: "Honor your father and your mother that your days may be long upon the land which the Lord your God is giving you" (Exod. 20:12).[3] This pivotal law initiates admonitions on relationships between people. In this context the law acts as the gateway to social strength paralleling in importance and role the message of the First Commandment: "You shall have no other gods before me." The position of the fifth injunction and its implied blessing indicates the high degree of reverence the statute enjoyed.

The word used for "honor your father and mother" comes from the root *kabad*. Its intensive form *(pi'el)* used here emphasizes the giving of "weight" to prominent people. It commonly refers to glorifying

God. The commandment states that children must grant full significance to parents even when they may be losing physical and economic indicators of importance. Honoring father and mother includes making them feel important for what they have achieved as parents and for what they have accomplished as the instructors of younger generations (Deut. 6:7, 20–21; 11:19).

Honoring parents includes treating as important those who are too feeble to demand respect in addition to giving significance to the strong and resourceful.[4] Children find it easy to prize successful parents in the prime of life who are enjoying the height of their wealth and productivity. But this command also requires adult children to treat as significant older parents who have stepped aside from their normal occupations. Growing older may enfeeble parents so that they become a burden and occasionally an embarrassment for their adult children. This commandment particularly challenges adult children to bestow honor on dependent parents.

Elderly parents normally require more "honoring" to keep their self-esteem alive. At this stage tasks easily accomplished in earlier years become somewhat problematic. Elders who begin the transition from provider to a more dependent role increasingly need more undergirding from the younger generation. Occasionally children find themselves dealing with role reversal in counseling ill and feeble parents. Elderly facing this transition of life especially appreciate children who prize them highly.

A promise in the Exodus version elaborates on the significance of the command to honor parents. The Decalogue incorporates the language of Deuteronomy[5] for its expansion. The promise combines two distinct elements: "That your days might be extended" and "upon the earth which the Lord (Yahweh) your God is giving you." In this way a promise out of common theology ("long life") joins with Israel's land theology to reinforce the relationship between Israel's behavior and God's gift of land. Such a promise also implies a similar threat: "Treating parents as insignificant will shorten your days in the land." That special relationship between treatment of parents and the welfare of the community is reinforced further by additional clauses within the law as it appears in Deuteronomy.

In Deuteronomy two motivational clauses reinforce parental honoring. They stress the quality of life attained therein and remind all that the command comes directly from the God of Israel (italics indicate expansions).

> Honor your father and your mother *so that it may go well with you*; that your days may be long,
>
> *as the Lord your God commanded you,* upon the land which the Lord your God is giving you. (Deut. 5:16)

The first motivation clause in the expanded form adds the promise of a good life to that of "lengthened" days. This clause states that obedience to this command brings divine blessings as well as continuing existence within the promised land. Implied within this promise is also an antithetical threat: "Violation of the honoring of parents produces hardship and difficulty that may lead to a premature loss of land with its good life." These motivation clauses clarify even more Israel's choice between blessings and curses, deliverance and punishment.

The second motivation clause mentions the law's divine authority assumed by the contractual context of the Exodus version. The addition categorically states the intense concern that the God of Israel feels about honoring parents. Deuteronomy reminds Israel that God personally decrees that parents be honored. This reminder focuses attention on the close personal relationship between God and the older generation.

Adjustments in Deuteronomy on the fourth law concerning the Sabbath indicate that the fourth and fifth laws at some time may have been elevated to a position of preeminence over the other commandments. Not only do they alone utilize a positive form in their statements, in Deuteronomy they together summarize Israel's kerygma of the exodus from Egypt and the giving of the land. Notice how verse 15 in the Sabbath commandment omits the creation motif prominent in the Exodus version (Exod. 20:11) and substitutes instead the theme of the exodus event:

> And you shall remember that you were a slave in the land of Egypt and the Lord your God brought you out from there by a mighty hand and an extended arm; therefore the Lord your God commanded you to keep the Sabbath day. (Deut. 5:15)

The prominence of Sabbath keeping in the postexilic community may provide some clue for the ultimate elevation of the two command-ments to the center of Israel's credo.

Israel's various themes of parental respect reach their apex of expression in the Holiness Code. Honoring parents is equated here with worship and awe. Priestly standards describing how Israel might become a holy people include this command as an introduction. Notice how this concern also unites parental respect with the require-ment of Sabbath keeping:

> Each of you should fear *(tiyra'u)* mother[6] and father and my sabbaths[7] you must keep. I am the Lord your God. (Lev. 19:3)

God's concluding expression of self-revelation of the holy name rein-forces the centrality of these commands.

Several points interest interpreters of this verse. First of all, the passage places fear of the mother before that of the father. Though the Greek translation of the Septuagint reverses this order, this unique passage remains in the masoretic text and is widely accepted as the earliest reading of the verse. The term used for fear normally refers to worship of God or a sense of awe at the divine power and majesty. Yet here the passage instructs children to feel awe for the most vulnerable parent first. Again the Bible reinforces in a rigorous manner filial responsibilities for honoring both father and mother.

Second, the verse teaches anew the theological importance of respect for parents. It places the command prior to Sabbath keeping in order and seals the passage with a divine disclosure formula. The terminology equates feelings for parents with those normally ex-pressed to God. In the context of this chapter, the command becomes the primary sign of a holy people. No doubt remains as to whether or not God supports the social structures that provide status and protec-tion for the elderly.

UNCONDITIONAL MANDATE FOR HONORING PARENTS AND ELDERS

Political and religious pressures during the Hellenistic period of Israel's history seem to have motivated the nation to consolidate and absolutize a number of traditional values. Under these pressures respect for old age and filial responsibilities of honor and obedience to parents rise to become unconditional mandates. Surviving literature from this period, the Apocrypha and Pseudepigraphia, indicates a standardized concern for such matters reaching a level of absolutism. Though the books of the Apocrypha vary widely as to style, content, and date, most share a heightened concern for the aging combining the shared common theology and unique emphases of Israel's earlier traditions.

Book of Wisdom

The Book of Wisdom, also called the Wisdom of Solomon, reflects themes from the common theology found in Proverbs and biblical wisdom literature. It both stresses respect for the elderly and challenges the older generation to pursue wisdom. The Book of Wisdom expresses concerns for the elderly that fit easily within the mainstream of the biblical message. It teaches that all should honor advanced age and recognizes that elderly are worthy of total respect.

On the other hand, in the tradition of Ecclesiastes the author recognizes that life is short, so he encourages the young to enjoy youth and carefully use each day (2:1–19). Only foolish youth use their vitality and strength as a license to show cruelty to whomever they wish. Only the foolish would show disrespect by oppressing the helpless and aging saying:

> Let us oppress the righteous poor
> Let us not spare the widow
> Nor *reverence* the old man's gray
> hairs full of years.[8]
> (Wisd. of Sol. 2:10)

The Wisdom of Solomon expresses agitated indignation over this attitude. It warns that an old age of dishonor plagues a foolish youth who might survive to that stage. The book teaches that foolishness eventually reaps its own punishment for breaches of God's standards.

> For evil ones, if they live very long, they shall be recognized as nothing and at the end in their old age shall lack honor. (Wisd. of Sol. 3:17)

In this way, the Book of Wisdom does not automatically equate old age with wisdom. Instead, the work stresses the importance of enjoying an "honorable old age." A good old age depends on a commitment to wisdom. Honor never is guaranteed to those who advance in years. An "honorable old age" must be earned. Long years lived in evil can lead to a grievous end.

> For honorable old age comes not so by means of length of time, nor is it measured by number of years; But understanding is gray hairs unto people, and an untarnished life is ripe old age. (4:8–9)

In that sense, a righteous youth can "quickly perfect the many years of an unrighteous man's old age" (4:16). Through wisdom anyone can enjoy honor with the elders, though that person might be young (8:10).

The Book of Wisdom clearly balances the common association of old age and wisdom with a concern for honorable and wise living. It stresses that only by wisdom standards can a person accomplish the goal of an "honorable old age." In this way it reinforces biblical warnings against foolishness and reminds all that aging provides no substitute for wise living.

Book of Sirach

The Book of Sirach, also called "The Wisdom of Ben Sira" or "The Proverbs of Ben Sira," provides an example of how by 200 B.C.E. the commandment "Honor your father and your mother" had grown in significance within the religious community. The book includes an exegetical expansion on the statute explaining the honoring of parents. Ben Sira's commentary presses for honor and service of parents by listing a number of possible blessings and curses. This passage further demonstrates the unique evenhandedness of Israel's traditions and raises the intensity of concern for filial responsibilities to a new level. Though again its message may be addressed to young, unmarried adolescents, its instruction likewise includes adults who deal with aged parents.

> Listen to me your father, O children;
> and act accordingly, that you may be
> kept in safety.

> For the Lord honored the father above the children,
> and confirmed the right of the mother over her sons.

> Whoever honors father atones for sins,
> and whoever glorifies mother
> is like one who lays up treasure.

Whoever honors father will be gladdened by
his/her own children,
and when that one prays he/she will be heard.

Whoever glorifies father will have long life,
and whoever obeys the Lord will refresh his/her mother;
that one will serve his/her parents as one would
masters.

Honor your father by word and deed,
that a blessing from him may come upon you.

For a father's blessing strengthens
the houses of the children,
but a mother's curse uproots their foundations.

Do not glorify yourself by
dishonoring your father,
for your father's dishonor is no glory to you.

For a person's glory comes from
honoring that one's father,
and it is a disgrace for children
not to respect their mother.

O child, help your father in his old age,
and do not grieve him as long as he lives;
even if he is lacking in understanding,
show forbearance;
in all your strength do not despise him.

For kindness to a father will not be forgotten,
and against your sins it will be credit to you;
in the day of your affliction it will
be remembered in your favor;
as frost in fair weather, your sins
will melt away.

Whoever forsakes his/her father is like a blasphemer,
and whoever angers his/her mother is cursed by the Lord.
(3:1–16)[9]

The sayings of Ben Sira clarify what it means to honor parents and lists the benefits of supporting them. They suggest that children atone for sins (3:3) and lay up treasure (3:4) by honoring parents. Attributing worth to parents insures safety (3:1), respect from one's own children (3:5), and forgiveness of sins (3:14–15). God's concern about the welfare of parents increases the strength of threats against those who disregard their filial duties. The Lord honors and confirms the status of parents (3:3, 6b), so much so that neglect or abuse of either parent makes one a "blasphemer" or "cursed by the Lord" (3:16).

No circumstances negate the command for filial support of parents. In the Wisdom of Sirach children must support and continue to respect parents even when they reach old age. Though an aging father may suffer under the effects of senility, still a child should not grieve or despise him but rather evidence patience and support for him (3:12–13). Truly, as Ben Sira says, the glory of a person comes out of unconditionally honoring and respecting parents (3:11).

In a more general way, the Book of Sirach also addresses the promises and problems of old age. Experience may be a good teacher (34:9–10), but wisdom and righteousness do not come automatically with eldership. Some become adulterers, lacking in sense (25:2; 42:8). Others, like a pious, wise scribe, leave an assured reputation whether living to old age or not (39:5–11). Old age comes as a gift from God (41:4), often by means of a good wife (26:27). The book warns that foolishness, envy, anger, and anxiety shorten one's days (27:25–29; 30:24). Through these teachings, the Book of Sirach presents a realistic view of both the respect due an elder (32:3) and the righteousness and piety such a person must epitomize.

Tobit

By telling a story the Book of Tobit also elevates filial honor and service to parents to an unconditional level. In the story, Sarah will not commit suicide after the death of her seventh husband (all deaths caused by a demon) out of concern for her father Reguel. She reaches a point of new courage as she thinks:

> Never shall they shame my father and say to him, "You had but one beloved daughter, yet she strangled herself because of her troubles!" And so I would bring down the white head of my father in grief to the grave. (3:10)[10]

Consideration for her father is her ultimate concern.

Tobias in the story represents an equivalent type of a faithful son. Tobit, his father, at age sixty-two becomes blind from a sparrow's droppings (2:10). Still, Tobias carefully listens to the charge of the weakened Tobit, who appears near death:

Bury me decently; and honor your mother; do not abandon her all the days of her life; do what is agreeable in her presence. Do not grieve her spirit in any matter. Be mindful of her, my boy, because many hazards did she incur for you in her womb; and when she is dead, bury her next to me in one grave. (4:1–4)

Tobias obediently replies: "All that you have commanded me I shall do, my father."

In a touching scene, Tobias's mother is concerned for his welfare as he faces danger and he is concerned about her grieving. Ultimately the story has a happy ending; the demon is disposed of and Tobias is able to bury both his father and his mother in honor.

And he sustained their old age in honor and buried them in Ecbatana of Media. (14:13)[11]

The story of Tobit teaches filial service and obedience in a manner similar to that used in later rabbinical stories. The debt of gratitude owed to a mother for bringing a child into the world clearly is pointed out as a primary motivation for filial obedience. Tobias's relationship with his parents represents an elevated form of biblical teaching weaving together both common and unique ideals of filial devotion.

Story of Aḥikar

The pseudepigraphal Story of Aḥikar[12] presents wisdom teachings delivered in proverbs and tales about the relationship between Aḥikar and Nadan. The book reinforces numerous oriental themes about honoring the wisdom of the aging. The teachings of Aḥikar also make some distinctive contributions that go beyond traditional emphases. Aḥikar absolutizes his advice to his adopted son Nadan with explicit blessings and curses. The tragic end of a disrespectful Nadan reinforces the unconditional nature of commands to honor parents and to listen carefully to the wisdom of the older generation.

[One who] despises father and mother "let that person die the death." The one who honors parents shall prolong days and life and shall see all that is good. (2:26, Arabic translation)

Common biblical passages instruct children to honor parents, but not to love them. However, a proverb of Aḥikar also contains an exception to this point. Reinforcing his teaching with a threat, a promise, and a comment about a debt of gratitude that children owe a parent, Aḥikar instructs Nadan with the suggestion:

Son, love your father who begat you, and incur not the curse of your father and mother, so that you may enjoy the prosperity of your sons. (2:78, Armenian)[13]

The tale of Aḥikar also describes intergenerational conflict and how that hurts the elderly. Nadan, the son of Aḥikar's sister, ignores advice from his aging teacher and undermines Aḥikar's reputation and authority by demeaning him with contempt and mockery, saying:

My father Aḥikar is grown old, and stands at the door of his grave; and his intelligence has withdrawn and his understanding is diminished. (3:1, Syriac)[14]

Truly, Nadan's search for power disrupts his relationship with his teacher. Unfortunately, Nadan rejects Aḥikar's command to honor and admire an aging person:

When you behold an aged man, you rise and stand up before him and magnify him. (2:80, Armenian)[15]

The Story of Aḥikar utilizes proverbs and a tale to reinforce biblical teachings on respect for the elderly. Proverbs illustrate how to treat the older person as sacrosanct and instruct younger persons to learn humbly from an experienced teacher. The tale reinforces the tenets of this common theology. For example, Aḥikar, the aged sage, speaks and acts discretely; Nadan, his sister's boy, portrays a foolish, deceptive youth who accepts negative stereotypes about aging. In clear terms the story shows that the words of Aḥikar offer life; the impudence of Nadan brings an early death. In addition to reinforcing the common theology and refuting popular stereotypes, however, Aḥikar uniquely stresses love for parents. Children through love may escape any fear of a parental curse. Filial love in turn insures for the child a future long life secure in the support of grateful children. In this way the Story of Aḥikar adds its own special variations to the common theology it absolutizes.

ESCHATOLOGY AND RESPECT FOR THE AGING

Eschatological passages from the prophets of Israel regard disrespect between generations as a sign of a degenerate people and indicators of the end of an old era. Prophets view uninterrupted aging and intergenerational respect as characteristics of the new kingdom era. They do not preach a message of youthful rebellion. Instead, prophets sharply rebuke impulsive tendencies in their younger generation. For example, Isaiah condemns their participation in oppression. Childish injustice in Israel's rulers seems abominable:

> And I will make lads their princes and capricious
> children to rule over them and the people will be
> oppressed, each one by one another and each one by a neighbor.
> The youth storm against the elder, and the inferior against the
>   honorable. . . .
> O my people! Their oppressors are children and women (mothers) rule
>   over them.
> O my people! Those who guide you lead (you) astray,
> And confuse the direction of your paths.
>
> (Isa. 3:4–5, 12)

A monarchy that oppresses those who represent traditional values and wisdom can expect the wrath of God and termination of its society.

The Book of Micah includes a passage in its latter chapters that describes the breakdown of trust between the generations. When Israel's society nears its extinction, honor and respect for parents will disappear. Consequently in those dark days the home loses its value as a sanctuary from enemies.

> For a son treats his father contemptuously
> Daughter rises up against her mother,
> Daughter-in-law against her mother-in-law,
> A person's enemies are the members of one's
> own household.
>
> (Mic. 7:6)

Such a society, Micah implies, deserves nothing except extermination. Insubordination demolishes the cornerstone of God's social structure—the family. In such an evil time the sin of Ham and Canaan against Noah conquers reason and respect. These are the signs that the last days of the old era have arrived.

In the new age, however, peace and security for all vulnerable generations becomes possible. Uninterrupted life will be insured. The third section of Isaiah (56—66) includes a vision of life in a reconstructed kingdom. This era finally offers the unaltered long life promised by a covenant blessing in the Book of the Covenant (Exod. 23:26):

No longer will there be an infant (who lives but a few days)
Or an old person who does not live out their days;
For the youth will die at the age of one hundred
And the one who does not reach the age of one hundred
Shall be thought accursed.

(Isa. 65:20)

Members of the rejuvenated people of God will enjoy a complete life
without interruption or danger in the new heavens and earth. The
ideal of old age according to this vision will become reality for all the
faithful.

In fact, a vision of the renewed city of truth in Zechariah rejoices
that both the elderly and the young again will fill the streets of
Jerusalem.

Thus says the Lord of Hosts,
Old men *(Z^eqenim)* and old women *(Z^eqenoth)*
will again sit in the streets of
Jerusalem, each one with staff in hand
because of (advanced) age *(merovh yamim)*
And the streets of the city will be
filled with boys and girls playing in
its streets.

(Zech. 8:4–5)[16]

According to an apocalyptic passage in Joel, every generation likewise will perform some important role at the outpouring of the Spirit
of the Lord during the messianic age:

I will pour out my spirit on all flesh;
And your sons and daughters will prophesy,
Your elderly will dream dreams,
Your youth will see visions.

(Joel 2:28; Eng.; 3:1 Heb.)

The return of Elijah mentioned at the close of Malachi once again will
unite the generations of the family:

And he will restore the hearts of the father to (their) children and the
hearts of the children to their fathers, lest I come and smite the land with
a curse. (Mal. 4:6)

Prophetic visions of the new age of reconciliation teach that the
social cornerstone of God's community once again will be restored.
Generation gaps will become creative and unifying forces as they

were created to be. Detrimental effects of expedience and narcissism finally will be corrected. Each generation will enjoy its own rightful place in God's new kingdom. Differences will blend to complete the marvelous new creation of society. No longer will strife and death be the enemies of peace and unity. The values of the elders will conquer those of monarchy. According to the realistic words of the prophets only a new era can fully implement the ideals of Israel's faith concerning care and honor for the elderly.

The blossoming of apocalyptic literature from 200 B.C.E. adds other dimensions to the concepts of aging. Elaborate visions of the new kingdom picture a triumphant almighty king, the "Ancient of Days" (Dan. 7:9, 13; 1 Enoch 46:1, 2; 47:3; 48:2; 71:10), seated on a throne, whose head is as white as lamb's wool.[17] The apex of strength clearly exhibits the chief characteristic of aging, white hair. White hair power reigns supreme in the messianic kingdom. In apocalyptic material the people of God and Jerusalem itself depend wholly upon the power of the Ancient of Days to subvert the dominant evil of the world and to establish a new era.

As in prophetic eschatology the Book of 1 Enoch[18] describes the social anarchy characterizing the end of the old era. As the heathen struggle against Jerusalem, they also will fight against one another. "A man does not know his brother, nor a son his father or mother."[19] The killing will be so intense that a father will kill his sons and his son's sons. Parents will abandon infants. Family respect and loyalties will collapse. Respect and obedience will cease to exist.

In contrast with that chaos, Apocalyptic books testify that the new era will reverse these signs of social and spiritual death. Purged from evil, the new earth will provide the proper environment for aging. The number of the living will be increased and in peace their years of joy will be multiplied:

> And then shall all the righteous escape, and shall live
> to beget thousands of children,
> and all the days of their youth and their old age
> shall they complete in peace.
>
> (1 Enoch 10:17)[20]

Apocalyptic materials expand on common prophetic themes while expressing alarm over the old era's disregard for life, parental respect, and family loyalties. They reiterate as well the possibilities of an unlimited life span in a world purged of sin and filled with peace. Old age in this sense is God's ultimate gift for members of the new messianic kingdom. Such a gift certainly fits the nature of the white-haired King of kings who desires the opportunity of white hair for all the righteous.

CREATION, ESCHATOLOGY, AND AGING

Apocalyptic pictures of the messianic kingdom anticipate fulfillment of the blessings of divine creation. The new creation complements and completes the goals and objectives of initial creation. An eschatological context finally makes possible the achievement of the full identity of humanity as proclaimed in the priestly materials (Gen. 1:26–30). Here human beings are said to be created in the "image of divinity, male and female." They are also granted dominion over the good world made by God.

The messianic kingdom in apocalyptic literature finally offers an opportunity for the faithful to dominate the earth. This context provides an environment of peace and security in which humanity can enjoy God's blessings without interruption. Creation provides humanity with the potential for growth, and aging indicates the achieving of this goal. White hair, like that gracing the head of the King of kings, represents the crowning achievement of the image of God. Hence, both creation and eschatology in the Bible add dignity and worth to old age.

CONCLUSION

Israel utilized a variety of commonly shared themes to teach respect for the aging. In its literature Israel added particular emphases and related its religious concepts to them. This mixture provided for points of difference between biblical teachings concerning the elderly and the teachings of surrounding cultures.

The unique faith of Israel taught concern for the elderly as a result of the just nature of God. Justice demanded deliverance for the vulnerable. The aging widow, the handicapped, or socially weakened parent all received special divine protection.

Concerns for honoring parents rose to new heights of evenhandedness and intensity in legal and wisdom traditions. In the Ten Commandments of Exodus negative concerns became positive proclamations. Similar commands equated such behavior with worship of God and Sabbath keeping. The texts attributed worth to parents and elevated filial respect to the forefront of human relationships and piety.

Glorifying old age and parents became an absolute value in the literature of the Hellenistic age. Children existed to care for the psychological and physical needs of aging parents. They owed a debt of gratitude to the one who gave them life that never could be repaid. To ignore that debt or the wisdom available through their instruction led to tragedy and an early end of life. Thus children became a means of God's blessings and support for the elderly.

Ultimately, only the new era as taught in eschatology, prophetic and apocalyptic, could bring intergenerational peace and respect to fulfillment. Then would all ambiguity and disrespect caused by competition and injustice be laid to rest. The image of God would be realized in the faithful. In this changed environment a long-sought-for unity could be fulfilled. A multiplicity of ages and roles would enrich the quality of life. Mutual honor and respect would be perfected at last when the messianic era completes the kingdom of God.

CHAPTER 6

Two Responses
to Respect for
the Elderly

Early Christianity and Judaism

Early Christian and Jewish literatures record how Israel's theology of aging impacted each community. Though each claims to have accepted Israel's Scripture as its own, each faith community also deals with aging issues in its own way. Nowhere do ideological similarities and differences appear clearer than in their particular approaches to commonly held attitudes toward the older generation. Each faith adds its own footnotes to the mandate to honor and respect parents and the elderly.

Documents from the first century C.E. indicate that Greco-Roman culture and laws also reinforced filial honor and obedience toward parents. Laws in Athens required that children maintain their aging parents.[1] Each family operated as a religious cult. Roman law elevated the authority of fathers through the rules of *patria potestas*.[2] These laws granted a father, as head of a family, absolute power over wife and children. To some degree early Christianity and Judaism were influenced by these common practices. This chapter will trace the threads that form a tapestry, a distinct response of each of these particular faiths to a common theology that absolutized filial honor and obedience to parental authority.

EARLY CHRISTIANITY AND
FILIAL OBEDIENCE

Christians in the first and second centuries C.E. respond to elevation of parental rights and filial submission in a variety of ways. One of the most puzzling aspects of their responses is a general silence on the matter of aging. Christian Scriptures rarely address the subject of respect for elders. Jesus and Paul speak passionately for human dignity, unity, and justice but hardly deal with aging issues.[3] This silence may indicate that Christianity largely shared the tenets of respect for the older generation assumed in most cultures of that period.

On the other hand, conflicts with prevailing cultures and within Christian communities at times compel Christianity to react against the dominance of society by the older generation and to modify some traditional assumptions. Under the pressures of beginning a new movement, Christians question some traditional first-century family values and radically reject unconditional submission to parental control and filial responsibilities. When normalcy returns and earlier crises no longer seem threatening, Christian writers propose solutions much closer to those of the traditional common theology. Diverse views in these texts preserve for subsequent generations tensions felt by early believers who tried to balance both religious and family responsibilities.

The Jesus Movement

The Jesus event produced a movement and a body of teachings that radically challenged many religious and social values of first-century Palestine. As might be expected, traditional institutions resisted the erosion of control threatened by this movement. These innovations directed this movement's struggle for acceptance against entrenched social and religious pressures. This turmoil, however, siphoned off energy for dealing with social responsibilities and specifically with the issues of aging.[4]

Later in the history of the Christian movement a preoccupation with the immediate arrival of the kingdom of God seems to have subsided. Epistles and other writings teach values related to a more settled life style. Social comments in these texts indicate that Christians finally felt more at ease in utilizing many values of the ancient traditions, and elements of their communal and social structures. In this context the epistles discuss relationships with the aging and family prescriptively.

To deal adequately with issues of aging in early Christian writings, biblical theology must balance those teachings that refer to a period anticipating the imminent arrival of the kingdom with those prescribed for a more stable relationship to the world. Absolutizing either radical innovations or traditional affirmations of parental authority can only distort the intent of these passages. Proclamations of "newness" correctly remain in tension with the more traditional social concerns of the epistles. Sensitivity to changing social contexts in early Christianity deeply enhances the interpretation of different texts.

The Synoptic Gospels and Acts

Passages in the Synoptic Gospels and Book of Acts contain few direct references to the transitions of life or aging. Crises of the new kingdom dominate their concerns. Their perspectives assume a religious and social context different from that of the epistles. Nevertheless, a study of attitudes and practices toward the elderly in the Synoptic Gospels provides a helpful background for comparing and contrasting their viewpoints with other books.

The evangelists picture Jesus as one who generated severe opposition from Jewish adherents to popular traditions and practices. He is said to propose innovations on ancient *(archaios)* teachings believed to have originated in both oral and written form with Moses. Quite naturally Jewish leaders in Palestine would resist changes in the venerable "traditions of the elders" (Mark 7:3, 5).

Jesus counters the authority of ancient traditions with a personal claim: "But I say unto you . . ." Jesus modifies the sacred *toroth* which was "said of old" (Matt. 5:21, 27 t.r., 33) with a new ethic of an imminent kingdom. The Gospels claim that even prophets of the distant past (Luke 9:8, 19) could not be compared with this new fearless proclaimer.[5] For the disciples the authority of their Messiah surpasses that of traditions from ancient times.[6]

The Synoptic Gospels, therefore, generally view ancient traditions in a negative light. They often caricature older traditions by using a word *(palaios, palaiotes, palai)* that refers to something "old, obsolete, antiquated, or outworn." The arrival of a new messiah in their opinion makes earlier dogma as obsolete as a worn-out garment and therefore must be replaced. This word ably fits the apologetical purposes of the Synoptic Gospels and the earliest preaching of the Christian community.

For example, Christian texts describe fasting as performed by the disciples of John and the Pharisees as a practice that must await the departure of the bridegroom. In addition, the Gospels suggest that practices such as fasting are like an old, worn-out coat or wineskin (Matt. 9:16, 17; Mark 2:21, 22; Luke 5:36, 37, 39). The grafting of traditional requirements such as fasting onto the message of the kingdom destroys its usefulness. For this reason, believers must discard such practices. Luke even adds that "old teachings" attract with a seductive power and hence must be resisted (Luke 5:39).[7]

The Synoptic Gospels' polemic against traditions they call old and obsolete should be interpreted in light of Christianity's early struggle for followers. Ancestral traditions would seem very attractive to persons steeped in the attitudes of ancient cultures. Consequently, the Gospels devalue these teachings by calling them worn-out in order to promote their new movement.

Gospel passages do not use consistently the word "old" *(palaios)* as a negative category. Matthew and Luke in passages about the kingdom of heaven modify their own devaluation of ancient teachings and even express some appreciation for older traditions that do not lose their value. For example, Matthew records a saying about the kingdom of heaven that states that every scribe who becomes a disciple of the kingdom of heaven puts forth both new and old *(palais)* treasure like a house master (Matt. 13:52). Luke suggests that the kingdom is like a bag (purse) that does not wear out with old age *(palaioumena)*. One should sell everything to enjoy its unfailing, heavenly treasures (Luke 12:33). Such statements warn interpreters against making generalizations about "old" traditions as if age lessens their value.

Though the Synoptic Gospels reject parts of the traditions of the elders, Luke demonstrates that the Gospels do not reject elders themselves or old age in general. Birth narratives in Luke record events centering on faithful elderly persons who anticipate and joyfully welcome the infant Messiah. Elizabeth and Zechariah, the aging parents of John the Baptist, represent a good case in point (Luke 1:18–25).

Luke also tells of Simeon, a God-fearing person facing death (Luke 2:25–35). He recognizes that the child Jesus is the promised one who will bring about the "salvation of people in Israel." Likewise, Anna, a prophet and widow of at least eighty-four years of age, thanks God for the child (Luke 2:36–38). Her old age does not keep her from becoming an early witness of the Messiah. These positive images of older people show that the Synoptic Gospels do not demean old age when they reject the doctrines of ancient traditions.

Followers of Jesus and participants in the life of the new movement seem to have experienced some turmoil because of family loyalties. Materials describing family life in Jewish communities of the first century show how the family promoted social cohesion.[8] People in that era appear to have lacked social mobility. Sons were to marry and bring their wives to live either inside their parents' house or adjacent to it. Parents arranged marriages and organized the future of their children.

Early followers of Jesus are reported to have responded to a millenarian[9] message. In this proclamation a new era is intersecting the present. Disciples are asked to forsake all former alliances and proclaim the message of the kingdom at any cost (Luke 14:33). Jesus calls believers to live in a style approximated by the term "wandering charismatics."[10] Such leave family, obtain their direction from the Spirit of God, and submit themselves to the authority of their leader. Normative social structures lose their significance.

A millenarian movement rarely addresses issues such as growing old and normative relations with parents. Mark and Q (material in common to Luke and Matthew) especially recommend a separated life style.[11] These teachings assume that the new era could arrive at any instant. Believers are to discard relationships that interfere with proclaiming the message of the kingdom. They are to live an itinerant life style (Mark 6:6–13; Luke [Q] 10:1–16).

In this spirit, Jesus in the Synoptics calls followers to free themselves of normal family ties:

> If anyone comes to me and does not hate father, mother, wife and children, brothers, sisters and besides them also life itself, such cannot be my disciple. (Luke [Q] 14:26)

Family ties interfere with a believer's availability, so one must discard them. A disciple's loyalty to the kingdom and to Jesus supercedes all other attachments.

The Synoptics also mention another practical reason for shedding family ties. Strained family relationships at times provoke severe persecution for believers who accept the stark, alternative kingdom. Loyalty to Jesus could bring a sword to families:

> Sons set against their fathers, daughters against their mothers, daughters-in-law against their mothers-in-law. A person's worst enemies will be members of one's own family. (Matt. 10:34–35; Luke 12:51–53; cf. Mic. 7:6)

Consequently, the Synoptic Gospels demand that discipleship consist of loving Jesus more than father or mother, son or daughter (Matt. 10:36). Literally applied, this radical loyalty would strain family relationships and alienate such wandering itinerant messengers from their communities (Matt. 10:5–20).

Jesus in the Synoptic Gospels lives out the role of an itinerant messenger. Luke describes him at age twelve remaining in Jerusalem independent of his parents to be in his "father's house" (Luke 2:41–49). In adulthood he becomes a wandering, homeless preacher of the kingdom. As would be expected, his family comes to get him, perhaps thinking he is crazy. All three Synoptics use the moment to emphasize one important aspect of discipleship. Believers assume the roles of mother, brother, and sister of the faithful, replacing actual family members (Mark 3:31–35; Matt. 12:46–50; Luke 8:19–21; cf. also Luke 18:28–30).

Jesus' millenarian teachings on the surface appear to justify family neglect, alienation, and filial insubordination. Certainly Luke counteracts this tendency by recording that though Jesus left his parents to remain temporarily in his father's house in Jerusalem, he later returns home with them during those early years (Luke 2:51). Likewise, Jesus chastises the Pharisees for using a religious vow of Corban as an excuse not to provide for elderly parents. In this context Jesus is disputing with Pharisees about his disciples' eating food with unclean hands. These experts of the law use the traditions of the elders to criticize Jesus' disciples. Jesus in turn uses the traditions of the elders to point out their own inconsistent treatment of their parents (Mark 7:5–13). To emphasize his concern for vulnerable adults, Jesus shows special sympathy for the plight of widows in his parables and teachings (Luke 4:25–26; 7:11–17; Mark 12:41–44; Luke 21:1–4). Likewise, as he interrogates the wealthy young ruler, Jesus includes "Honor your father and mother" in his list of crucial behaviors and responsibilities (Mark 10:19).

Why in the Synoptic Gospels does Jesus command disciples to leave their families? In an era inaugurating the impending kingdom all believers need the freedom to concentrate on preaching the gospel. Pressures from defensive and resistant families certainly would cause great hardships for believers.[12] Defensive families would reject and persecute intinerant family members who break with kinship norms and society to follow Jesus (Mark 13:12–13). In the Gospels only disciples who resist family pressures to the end would enter the kingdom (Mark 13:13b).

Despite emphatic warnings against family obstruction, the Synoptic Gospels do not advocate abandonment of family responsibilities. Rather, they particularly stress total allegiance to the proclamation of the gospel. Additional teachings in the Gospels balance family concerns with radical demands for discipleship. The full message of the Synoptic Gospels leaves both viewpoints in tension. In this sense the Synoptic Gospels alter common support for an unconditional mandate of filial obedience and yet reaffirm in general the importance of such behavior when possible.

Elders *(presbyteroi)* appear in the Synoptic Gospels as powerful officials in the religious establishment.[13] The Gospels generally portray elders as officers who unite with Pharisees, Sadducees, teachers of the law, and scribes to oppose Jesus and to defend the interests of the religious status quo. Some elders even act as members of the Sanhedrin (Matt. 16:21; 26:3 t.r.; 27:41; Mark 8:31; 4:27; 14:43, 53; 15:1; Luke 9:22; 20:1). Only an elder leading a local synagogue does not oppose Jesus (Luke 7:3). The Gospels do not view eldership as a legitimate national office deserving honor and obedience. Instead, the evangelists type the elders of Israel as self-serving agents of a structure opposed to the new Jesus movement. They conclude that elders who neglect their legitimate function as defenders of the rights of the people disqualify themselves from their deserved respect.[14]

Acts types the elders of Israel in a way similar to that used by the synoptic writers. Opponent elders generally reject and persecute the infant movement of Christianity (Acts 4:5; 8:23). Only Gamaliel fulfills the traditional role of elder and allows the movement time to demonstrate its genuineness (Acts 5:34–39). The rest are portrayed as executing Stephen (Acts 6:12) and plotting against Paul (Acts 23:14; 24:1; 25:15).

On the other hand, Acts chronicles the rise of a Christian structure of eldership and governance similar to that found in a local synagogue council.[15] A council of elders directs the church in Jerusalem (Acts 11:30; 21:8). Paul and Barnabas appoint elders wherever they travel (Acts 14:23). In Ephesus Paul assembles elders to hear his farewell address (Acts 20:17).

Apostles and elders together apparently lead the church in Jerusalem. They assume the authority to settle disputes within the Christian movement arising out of gentile growth (Acts 15:2, 4, 6, 22, 23).[16] Such decisions are said to appear under the title "rules of the apostles and elders in Jerusalem" and carry some authority for other churches (Acts 16:4).

In Acts Christian eldership represents the best in church leadership. Acts contrasts the attitudes of the elders of Israel with those of an emerging Christian leadership. Realizing that both sides depend on elders for leadership helps the interpreter understand better Christian statements against opposition elders. Such do not imply disrespect for their old age. Instead, disagreements with the elders of Israel issue mainly out of their categorical rejection of the new movement. Acts and the Gospels affirm the leadership role of older persons but at the same time reject the authority of opponent elders and the social structures they represent. In their place, Acts chronicles the rise of a more sympathetic social structure within the Christian movement which will displace the leadership of the elders of Israel.

Old Age in the Pauline Letters

A more stable relationship to its social context encouraged the Christian movement in parts of its developing literature to address issues of family responsibilities. As a result some epistles bearing the imprint of Paul deal sympathetically with strained family relationships. Though some passages treat old age in a polemical manner, other portions express concern about neglect of filial respect and obedience. These epistles generally affirm Israel's common theology on intergenerational respect and yet add balance to its requirements.

Passages in Pauline epistles, like those in the Synoptic Gospels, use the word "old" in polemics against evil. Age becomes a useful category for allegories against sin and immorality. "Old yeast" must be eliminated from the "new Passover bread" for it represents sin and immorality (1 Cor. 5:7–8). Christians now should celebrate the Passover with Christ the Passover Lamb and unleavened bread free from the "old yeast of sin and immorality."

Romans also utilizes the word "old" as a synonym for evil by stating that "our old person" *(palaios)* must be "crucified" that believers might not be slaves of sin (Rom. 6:6). The letter contrasts the useless "old way" *(palaiotetos)* of living under the guidance of a "written law" with following the new way of the Spirit (Rom. 7:6). Two passages from Ephesians and Colossians also identify the old self with sinful desires (Eph. 4:22; Col. 3:9). Putting away "old ways" brings salvation. The gift of a "new self" recreates a person in the likeness of God. Such texts demand adequate explanation lest they be misunderstood.

For example, an old, sinful nature should not be confused with an aging body or older psyche. The antithesis of an old nature does not include following a youthful or modern life style. "New" life in purity and truth may be obtained by both young and old. The message of these passages offers intergenerational hope. Properly understood, such promises may unite age groups, not divide them. Contrasts between "old" and "new" may be interpreted more accurately by recognizing the polemical style of the passages and by not confusing "old" with postmature years.

In fact, Paul seems oblivious to concern about intergenerational conflict. Consider his omission of this in his list of societal divisions (Gal. 3:28–29). Evidently, relationships between the young and the old seem satisfactory to him. At least, he does not feel that societal attitudes warrant any statement about them. He treats family relationships with some concern, but generally supports the social structures that affirm the importance and leadership of older members of society. For this reason, it can be assumed that parts of the current common theology of aging remained integrated within early Christianity.

Colossians and Ephesians

Passages from Colossians and Ephesians indicate a more family-oriented way of life. No longer does proclaiming the gospel divide families to the extent assumed in the Synoptic Gospels. The epistles instruct disciples to live not as itinerant messengers but rather as responsible members of a marriage and a family as exemplified by Jesus' relationship with the church. Such social statements reflect a return to some form of family normalcy in the Christian community and an interest in Christians abiding at least minimally by common social standards and perhaps even surpassing them.

Admonitions appear in Colossians and Ephesians concerning family relationships and duties. The so-called house-tables[17] list rules reflecting acceptable patterns for household behavior. These describe "station codes,"[18] offering a guide for each station of life. However, since this discussion deals with aging concerns, it focuses on codes relating children to parents (Col. 3:20–21; Eph. 6:1–4). These verses best illustrate rising family tensions between the generations.

The lists in these two passages are addressed primarily to children who may be neither young nor dependent.[19] These commands for filial duty reinforce their demands for filial duty with adult motivational clauses: "In the Lord, for this is right" (Eph. 6:1); and "For it is pleasing in the Lord" (Col. 3:20). A quote in Ephesians of the fifth commandment with its promise "so that it might go well with you and you may live a long time in the land" (Eph. 6:2–3) confirms that the passages primarily instruct adults. In this way the passages follow the ancient world view that offspring are obligated to filial respect and service as long as they live.

Children who outgrow fear of parental reprisal especially need religious sanctions to motivate them to "obey" *(hypakouete)* and "honor" *(tima)* parents. They require strong moral injunctions to impress them with the seriousness of filial violations and to guide them to moral rightness. The family code in Colossians particularly encourages children to obey parents because such behavior pleases God as well as their parents. In this sense the passages sanction filial obedience with divine promises and exhortations as does the common theology.

The *Haustafeln* (household codes) also teach clearly that filial obligations absolutely bind all children for life. Faithful offspring obey both powerful and feeble parents, even when they may be losing their strength. The passages provide recognition for those whose normal status may be slipping. Ephesians and Colossians move beyond the principles of voluntary submission. The verses command offspring to do what parents ask them to do. Such obedience secures respect which parents of all ages cherish but which aging ones especially desire. Filial service and religious devotion in that context provide a social structure for cushioning the mental and social anguish of aging.

As in earlier biblical statements about parental respect, the *Haustafeln* show equal concern for both father and mother. The passages display no partiality for the father to the loss of the mother. Evenhanded consideration is particularly crucial for the aging mother or widow. These epistles join the common theology of the ancient Orient in challenging children to grant their mothers filial obedience and expressions of honor.

The *Haustafeln* in Ephesians and Colossians add one variation which sets their statements apart from other unconditional mandates for filial obligations. These epistles also command fathers to treat their children with respect and compassion. In a Roman society dominated by *patria potestas,* where a father enjoys unlimited power over an offspring, it is important that these passages limit the power of fathers and warn them against abusing their authority (Eph. 6:4; Col. 3:21).

Colossians limits paternal authority by requiring that fathers not irritate their children (Col. 3:21). The literature of Judaism contains numerous examples of parents who provoke or irritate their children through irresponsible, irrational demands. Such an abuse of obedient offspring causes timidity, despondency, and a poor self-image (the losing of heart) for children. Nagging and extreme criticism as well as physical abuse constitute biblical forms of child abuse. Even a lack of positive reinforcement from fathers brings discouragement for children. The Colossians list encourages fathers to interact with their children in a way conducive to developing a healthy self-image.

Ephesians presents an even clearer admonition to fathers (6:4). The dispenser of discipline must control his power; abuse of his privileges only makes offspring angry. As the epistles command children to obey parents, so they balance this concern by instructing parents to consider the feelings of children.

The *Haustafeln* in both Colossians and Ephesians give unique suggestions for lessening tensions between the generations. In a balanced fashion they instruct both parents and children to treat each other as honored people. These guidelines add a variation of their own to more absolute admonitions concerning parents and children. Jew and

Christian alike can recognize the wisdom of these guides for all "stations of life."

Pastoral and General Epistles

Concerns within the pastoral and general epistles present a remarkably uniform picture. The increasing incidence of teachings about widows and older leaders indicates an aging population in the early church. As the church leadership ages it needs more support. Unfortunately certain younger church members appear to be heavily criticizing some of the elders. These epistles deal with such aging crises by restating the principles of obedience and honor, reinforcing them with strong religious threats and motivation clauses. In this way the materials reflect anew what has become a Christian form of the common theology on aging and family responsibilities.

While the pastoral and general epistles do not describe a fully developed presbytery system similar to that which appears in postapostolic writings,[20] these materials do mention elders who act as leaders in the churches. The pastoral epistles of Timothy and Titus describe a body of leaders who bestow spiritual gifts on young church members through prophecy and the laying on of hands (1 Tim. 4:11–14). Such "elders" enjoy some official position, financial support, and authority, for Timothy deems "elders who rule well" as worthy of "double honor" and "worth their hire" (1 Tim. 5:17–18). Congregational members are not to accuse them of wrongdoing unless they can support the charge with two or three witnesses (1 Tim. 5:19–20). Titus, likewise, describes similar leaders who function as church overseers (Titus 1:5–9). The epistle commands that Titus appoint (ordain) elders in every community (Titus 1:5) as did Paul (2 Tim. 1:6). The passage directly equates such an office with that of bishop or overseer in title, task, and requirements (Titus 1:6–9; 1 Tim. 3:1–3). Nothing specific in the text directly states that elders must be older, but it is implied by the dual meaning of the term *presbyteroi* (Titus 1:5).

Second, other passages in the pastoral epistles address elders as older persons and deal with society's attitudes toward aging. In 1 Timothy 5 a young leader is ordered not to rebuke an older man (*presbyteros,* 1 Tim. 5:1). Instead, the younger should encourage an elder by granting him the respect and honor of a father. This younger leader also is commanded to treat younger men as brothers, to honor older women *(presbyterai)* as mothers, and to respect in purity younger women as sisters (1 Tim. 5:2).

Next, Timothy deals with aging issues by discussing "giving" support to widows. Widows with living children should be taken care of by them. Adult children should support their widowed mother motivated by religious duty and a sense of gratitude. Such care pleases God (1 Tim. 5:3–4). A person who does not care for such dependents denies the faith and is "worse than an unbeliever" (1 Tim. 5:8). When does a widow without any children qualify for church support? She must be sixty years old, have been married only once, be a good mother, possess a reputation for good deeds, and have performed many kind services (1 Tim. 5:9–10). Younger widows should remarry instead of receiving assistance from the church (1 Tim. 5:14). The ideal solution, however, is for believers (male or female) themselves to take care of a widow and not burden the church (1 Tim. 5:16). Such care indicates that at this stage in the life of the church a concern for social structures like that of the common theology of aging now dominates church practices.

By the time of the writing of the pastoral epistles congregations seemed to be more selective about which widows they helped. This indicates a shift from earlier charismatic days in Jerusalem when all believers shared as a family their possessions and distributed them to those in need including the widows (Acts 6:1–6). The social structure of the Christian community here is developing into a Christian form of the defensive kinship and marriage model.[21] Support and affection now come through the kin group which as a unit shares a common religious motivation (1 Tim. 5:11–16). Life herein is more family-centered so the family now assumes the major load of care for the weak and needy. The experiment of the church in Jerusalem is replaced by a more normative family support system.

Eldership in the rest of 1 Timothy 5 primarily describes a church leadership position. Such leaders who speak and teach should be honored, paid, and not accused of a sin without adequate witnesses (1 Tim. 5:17–20). This protection of elders frees these church leaders to warn others of sin. Since the position is sacred, eldership should not be granted without long reflection. Therefore, the epistle warns: "Be of no hurry to lay hands on anyone for the Lord's service"

(1 Tim. 5:22). Before eldership, Christian leaders ought to demon-strate for a period of time a maturity level adequate to lead the congregation in a life of purity (1 Tim. 5:22). While Timothy may not directly state that old age is a requirement for church leadership, the letter does suggest that leaders possess a measure of maturity which comes with age and experience.

In the Epistle to Titus also, elders are addressed as older men *(presbytas)* and women *(presbytidas)*. The letter challenges Titus to teach older men and women to live as exemplar models for the younger generation (Titus 2:2–8). Elderly men first need to learn to be "temperate, worthy of respect, self-controlled and sound in faith, in love and endurance" (Titus 2:2). Older women need to live a reverent life, not being slanderous or addicted to alcoholic beverages, and to teach what is good (Titus 2:3). Then both can teach younger generations the life style they need to become loving, self-controlled, and pure persons.

Again the Epistle to Titus describes the leadership responsibilities of the older generation. They are to act as the teachers of the younger generation and models of the Christian life style so that no one malign the "word of God" or condemn its adherents (Titus 2:5–8).

No thoughts of retirement from church leadership are implied in this text. Instead, elderly members remain a key to the success of the Christian movement. Old age brings some transitions but decreasing responsibility is not one of them. Instead, the reputation of the Christian movement depends on their examples, teaching, and soundness of speech. Titus suggests that soundness in these areas alone will silence those who would say something bad about the new movement (Titus 2:8b).

Within the general epistles, 1 Peter stresses a household concept of relationships between the generations.[22] Such responsibilities again are reciprocal for the household of God. That section begins with a statement appealing to church elders from "one who is an elder himself" (1 Pet. 5:1). As an elder the author speaks as one who has been a witness to the past events of Jesus' suffering. On the authority of this eldership, the author appeals to other elders to work as willing shepherds with a desire to serve. As the *Haustafeln* warn fathers to consider the feelings of their children, so 1 Peter commands elders not to rule over a flock but rather to lead by example (1 Pet. 5:3–4).

In the same way the epistle commands younger men to submit themselves to the elders. The passage teaches submission *(hypotagete)* to the leadership of the older elders *(presbyterois)* as if the young are wearing an apron of humility (1 Pet. 5:5). The epistle supports no youth movement to displace older leaders. Rather, the passage reinforces the submission of younger members to their elder leaders by quoting a motivational maxim, "Because God resists the arrogant but gives grace to the humble" (1 Pet. 5:5c; cf. Prov. 3:34). Good reciprocal relations between the generations may be accomplished by elders who "shepherd willingly," not "exercising lordship" *(katakurieuantes)*, and when youthful members "submit" themselves to the authority of older leaders and in humility to one another. Responsibility rests on both generations to imitate this wise instruction.

In contrast to the ambiguity of other references to elders, the Epistle of James clearly describes eldership as a church office. The letter mentions local elders who pray over and anoint the sick with oil. As a result, their prayer made in faith could restore the sick to health and forgive sins (James 5:14–15). Such a group may be primarily older members but does not exclude mature younger ones. Elders function here as spiritual leaders. More than likely the term "church elders" used by James refers to those holding a local eldership office, the exact composition of which remains unknown.

In the pastoral and general epistles concern for an aging congregation generates more guidelines about the Christian family's obligation to support feeble and helpless elderly. The congregation no longer offers all widows direct aid. Instead passages admonish families in this era to take care of their own members. At the same time a new generation of church members is challenging the leadership of older members. The positions of aging elders need reinforcing so sections of the letters address this directly. Truly the passages indicate that ideals of reverence and honor are being strained by earlier Christian attitudes of ageism. Epistles of this era therefore marshal the ideals of God's close relationship with the elderly from Israel's teachings to restore church respect and support for the elderly. God supports the social structures of respect and obedience which provide security for older leaders. Likewise, God's concern for justice demands that Christian families and communities meet the needs of the most vulnerable of widows and that parents not violate the emotional needs of their children. In this way the epistles generally offer a variation on the common theology of aging that combines filial support with reciprocal responsibilites for the older generations.

Johannine Literature

The positive attitude of Johannine materials toward age and the elderly creates a pleasant sense of community. Polemical discussions of old traditions do not dominate the focus of this tradition. Instead the Gospel and letters assume a unity between the present and the past. Generations no longer seem divided. The older generation represents the fountainhead of the gospel of Christ. This literature places new Christian elders and their message about Jesus in a place of honor which they merit for devoted service to the cause. In this sense the literature reflects a full appreciation for the elderly and a developing Christian structure of the early centuries in the Common Era.

The Gospel of John, unlike the Synoptic Gospels, does not contrast the old with the new. Nothing in the material implies that age is undesirable. Old age does not imply that something, some tradition, or someone is out of date or worthless. For instance, the Gospel describes Jesus as the eternal word existing from the beginning with God (John 1:1). Likewise, in this material the Pharisee Nicodemus comes to Jesus by night to ask for advice (John 3:1–2). He seems upset when Jesus tells him that he must be born again. He is already mature and in his own words he has arrived at old age *(gerōn)*. Nevertheless, old age presents no block to his fulfillment. Jesus responds by teaching that even one who has aged can begin again by being "born of water and the spirit" (John 3:4–6). Age in this Gospel presents no barrier to eternal life or membership in the kingdom.

John teaches nothing about hating either family or parents. Family crises because of the gospel may be less of a problem by this time in the Johannine community. The Gospel also portrays the family circle of Jesus in a more normative fashion. John alone records that Jesus with his disciples and family attends the wedding of a friend of the family. Mary the mother of Jesus places enough faith in Jesus and his power to grant him complete control of a wine shortage for a wedding at Cana in Galilee (John 2:1–11). Even Jesus' mild rebuke does not discourage her faith in him (John 2:4).[23]

Unfortunately, the Gospel records that Jesus' brothers do not share this faith (John 7:5). Nevertheless, Jesus in this tradition does not struggle for independence from familial ties. Instead, at the cross, Jesus recognizes his filial duty and places his mother under the care of the disciple whom he loved (John 19:26–27). The family in Johannine tradition no longer appears as the enemy of the new kingdom.[24] Faith in Jesus within the Gospel of John enables all generations to enjoy loving, responsible family and intergenerational relationships within the Christian community.

John, like Matthew, states that ancient traditions may help one understand better the person of Jesus. Jesus argues in this Gospel that Moses wrote about him. Belief in Moses may lead to belief in Jesus (John 5:45–57). The Gospel refers to Israel's ancestors as "fathers" *(paterōn)*. In John Jesus marshals the teachings of Moses to defeat the "Jews" (John 7:19–24). No elders appear to argue with Jesus; the Gospel simply calls them "Jews."[25] To the contrary, in the independent text of John 8:9,[26] elderly bystanders (elders) first realize the truth of what Jesus says and leave before the rest. In every instance, these traditions treat elders and the elderly with respect and honor.

The Letters of John also view positively that which is older and earlier. Each Johannine epistle appears to cherish anew an earlier (older) gospel experience and message which now the Christian community accepts as ancient tradition. Speaking with a plurality of voices the first letter states that: "We write to you about a word which existed from the beginning" (1 John 1:1). In the First Epistle of John believers reiterate what they earlier experienced, saw, and heard. They speak as elders or preservers of an earlier tradition. They no longer consider their received tradition or Christian torah as new. These written teachings incorporate an "old command" *(entolen palaian)* or "message that you previously heard." This explanation of an earlier message incorporates a "new command" (John 13:34–35) whose truth Jesus formerly proclaimed. The message of the First Epistle of John applies anew an old gospel faithfully preserved by heirs of an earlier teaching.

In contrast to the Synoptic Gospels, distance from the Christ-event changes the perspective of this epistle. Now the writer repeats the new commandment of Jesus as an old commandment. An earlier tradition now becomes the basis for new insights for its successors. The epistle exegetes the earlier Gospel for a new context. In this epistle old and new attain a proper balance.

Second and 3 John confirm this view. The letter introduces the author as simply "the elder" *(presbyteros)* (2 John 1, 3 John 1). Current attitudes toward eldership eliminate the need for any reference to another type of authority. Eldership contains its own authority and prominence. Identification of the author as an elder places the person in the tradition of one who bears a message of the past and assumes leadership in the body of believers. Therefore the elder says: "This is no new command that I write you: it is the command which you have heard from the beginning" (2 John 5–6). The author addresses church members as "children" in the faith using tender, parental instruction. The elder speaks as one who incorporates the past and who wishes the best for younger Christians. Each letter of the elder represents a remarkable study of one who blends old aspects of the gospel with a fresh concern for the present. The letters certainly retain no depreciation of that which is old.

The Book of Revelation, like earlier eschatological and apocalyptic materials, includes elders and the elderly in its vision of a messianic kingdom. First, the coming Messiah, Jesus, arrives under a cloud cover and proclaims: "I am the Alpha and the Omega, who is, who was and who is to come." The description of the Messiah includes hair white as wool. The divine ruler proclaims: "I am the first and the last" (Rev. 1:7–17). Certainly this Christian apocalyptic vision of the Messiah reflects earlier images from Daniel and 1 Enoch and the enthronement of the Ancient of Days. The divine Messiah appears as an elderly person full of wisdom, power, and glory. White hair holds a significance that goes beyond even that of purity. The vision elicits awe at the sight of eternal glory (Rev. 1:17).

Later, twenty-four elders surround the throne of God, the magnificent ruler. They dress in white and wear gold crowns (Rev. 4:4). These elders worship the exalted one (Rev. 4:10), narrate salvation events (Rev. 5:5), sing songs (5:8–14), answer questions of the writer (4:13–17), pray for justice for the martyrs (11:16–18), listen to the new song sung by one hundred and forty four thousand redeemed from the earth (14:3), and pronounce the final "Amen, Praise God" (19:4) for the burning of Babylon. Adoration from prominent persons such as elders adds to the impression of power and might possessed by the eternal ruler.

Whatever the twenty-four elders represent, they truly fulfill honored roles as faithful leaders who celebrate the triumph of righteousness. Though the text mentions nothing about the age of the elders in these passages, the presbyter imagery lends itself to picturing older persons surrounding the throne of God. The significance of the elders does not change whether the actual number was inspired by astral concerns, twenty-four priestly divisions as in Chronicles (1 Chron. 25:9–31), twenty-four divisions of the tribes and districts, twenty-four books of the Hebrew Bible, or a combination of twelve tribes and twelve apostles.[27] Rather, the vision of elders gathered around the throne of God reminds Christians everywhere that older persons remain very significant members in the inner circle of God's kingdom. In the Apocalypse they represent the archetype of all leaders for the church. The value attributed to elders in the final consummation of the kingdom of God lends even more significance to the command: "Do not rebuke elders." Truly the Apocalypse reinforces common respect for aging leaders.

Apocalyptic material engenders hope for the suffering young and old by describing how a new era will break into history inaugurating a new heaven and new earth (21:1). Note, however, that contrary to the Synoptic Gospels the Apocalypse uses words to describe the former *(protas)* heaven and earth that imply that the earlier world was neither worthless nor worn out. Its terminology instead exalts the new era rather than degrades the former. Because the former *(prota)* era entailed pain for the martyrs, it must be replaced. With that triumph in mind the enthroned Savior proclaims: "It is done! I am the Alpha and Omega, the beginning and the end" (21:6). With this shout the Savior worshiped by the Christian community claims to be the origin of all things, the first and the last. The old and the new join together in the Christian vision of the messianic kingdom.

Conclusion

In a context of radical discontinuity the Synoptic Gospels recorded few direct, constructive guidelines for honoring the aged. Those that did appear, especially in Luke, provided some encouragement for the elderly. Older, faithful Palestinian Jews accepted the infant Jesus as the Messiah and rejoiced in a new era that his birth inaugurated. When normal family relationships were possible, however, Jesus condemned any shirking of duty toward aging parents and demonstrated open compassion toward the "curse of widowhood."

Intergenerational concerns minimized in the Synoptic Gospels were addressed thoroughly in the pastoral and general epistles. Their social contexts implied that a form of normalcy had returned to family life and church organization. Christian letters began to deal more with overcoming social problems associated with growing old. These epistles commanded all generations to care for one another and to accept reciprocal responsibilities toward each other. They reinforced filial duties toward parents with the authority of divine promises. Support and honor given to parents pleased the Lord and was right.

Early Christian churches, like the synagogues of Judaism, continued to identify leadership with eldership. Aging in the Christian community did not necessarily bring a loss of status or responsibility. In some way responsibilities increased as physical stamina decreased. Older members were challenged to live exemplary lives for the younger members to imitate. Christian materials did not mention any point of retirement from duties or any undue relinquishing of responsibility. Instead, their teachings reinforced the authority of the elders and called for mutual, reciprocal respect for and service from the generations.

The passages that included negative references to old age have been carefully scrutinized and interpreted. The Synoptic Gospels, following the lead of Mark, identified old age with traditions by which Israel rejected Jesus. Luke and Matthew modified this message somewhat but also retained the view that the ancient traditions of the elders remained useless and antiquated. Paul allegorized the old as representing the ways of sin and immorality. In his epistles the new creation of God's grace reversed the detrimental results of the "old gospel."

The Johannine literature reminded interpreters that the Bible did not demean "old" per se, whether the word "old" pertained to ancient traditions or to aging people. The Gospel and epistles of John recorded a message of an eternal Word which represented an "old" gospel of "the elder." The Johannine community valued highly this "old commandment."

As Christian literature that came to be known as the New Testament has demonstrated, the movement gathered its own traditions which likewise became precious to its followers. Old traditions about Jesus became as valuable as the aging leaders who transmitted them. These aging leaders in the community inspired younger believers so much so that elders were pictured celebrating around the throne of God at the inauguration of the new era.

The teaching and practices of early Christianity provided ample reminders that God's blessings for the elderly remained intact. God legitimized Christian families and church structures as vehicles for supporting the needs of older persons. God's concern for justice and order demanded filial obedience and honor for aging parents. These teachings balanced intergenerational relationships by providing an environment of mutuality and loving reciprocity.

In this way Christian literature moved from conflict with the absolutization of filial obligations in the Synoptic Gospels to an affirmation of family responsibilities. In a more normal familial context Christian epistles emerged from that process with a modified version of the common theology balanced by mutual respect and support. Ultimately Christian literature such as the Johannine materials reaffirmed the dignity of old age and elevated elders by promoting respect for them and praising their leadership.

RESPONSE OF EARLY JUDAISM TO
COMMON AGING VALUES

Sacred documents of Judaism reflect also general values similar to those of ancient oriental societies elevating old age and filial obligations. That consensus appears in meager teachings on the subject in Mishnah tractates, their commentaries, and related Talmuds. These documents reinforce the common theology of Israel and at the same time make some distinctive adjustments.

For example, devotion to parents is an important value to the moralists and jurists whose sayings are recorded in the Talmud and Mishnah. These traditions cherish filial respect similar to that of the Roman *patria potestas* and illustrate how an adult child should respond respectfully to parental provocations. Such materials support obedience to elders in halakhic examples or stories with a moral and thereby support current social structures.

How widely Jewish circles actually practiced respect for elders as taught in the *halakhoth* can never be ascertained with precision. However, consistency and uniformity of beliefs in Judaic literature supporting the elderly and filial obligations point toward a general acceptance of these ideals. Truly, insights from early rabbinical literature reflect a widespread Jewish ethos of support for elders that stretches back in some cases to the close of the second century c.e.

Mishnah

Support for the importance of older leaders appears in traditions discussing the origin of Jewish sacred books. The Mishnah describes itself and its commentaries as the heritage of the elders. Talmudic collections of *halakhoth* are said to be the product of elders or rabbinical teachers. A legend concerning the transmission of the so-called Torah states that Moses passed instruction to Joshua who in turn gave it to the "Elders" (Josh. 24:31). Prophets finally are said to have delivered this heritage to the men of the Great Synagogue.[28] No wonder the "traditions of the elders" stress the value of elderly leadership and thereby support the social structures that provide stability and significance for them.

Rabbinical literature also supports the elderly because they are identified with great wisdom. From Hillel the elder to Rabbi Judah the Patriarch, the traditional editor of the Mishnah, teachers equate old age with an endowment of understanding.

> As R. Eleazer said to Azariah: "Lo, I am like to one who is seventy years old, yet failed to understand (prove) why the going forth from Egypt should be rehearsed at night. . . . " (Berakhot 1:5)[29]

Wisdom is so associated with old age that extraordinary knowledge could make one seem to be seventy years old even if one were still young.

In addition, the Mishnah, in a list of ages and characteristics for the transitions of life, isolates age and experience as key ingredients for leadership.

Age	Characteristic
40 yrs.	discernment
50 yrs.	counsel
60 yrs.	eldership
70 yrs.	gray hair
80 yrs.	special strength
90 yrs.	bowed back
100 yrs.	as one who has already died (Avoth 5:27)

Since the Mishnah suggests that a person becomes an elder at age sixty, it is clear that it views age and leadership as virtually synonymous.

Undoubtedly in practice some rabbinical elders seem to have been younger than sixty years of age when they attained eldership. Some inherit their position. Others, such as Rabbi Eleazer, are outstanding scholars who are accepted as elders in their youth. Nevertheless, literature of that era normally associates eldership with old age. In this way Mishnaic passages legitimate leadership roles that ancient society bestowed upon the elderly.

Old age in Jewish literature remains a sign of God's blessing and a delight to its recipients. Along with other signs of success it is prized by the righteous and the world in general. Yet famous Jewish teachers also recognize that age does not necessarily indicate wisdom.

R. Simeon ben Judah in the name of R. Simeon ben Yohais said:

> He that learns as a child, to what is he like?
> To ink written on new paper.
> He that learns as an old man, to what is he like?
> To ink written on paper that has been blotted out.

R. Jose b. Judah of Kefar ha-Babi said:

> He that learns from the young, to what is he like?
> To one who eats unripe grapes and drinks wine from
> his winepress.
> And he who learns from the aged, to what is he like?
> To one who eats ripe grapes and drinks old wine.

Rabbi (Judah) said:

Look not on the jar but on what is in it; there may be
a new jar that is full of old wine
And an old one in which is not even new wine.
(Avoth 4:25–27)

For example, the first passage in isolation reflects an aging stereotype where the young easily learn and older people learn only with difficulty. However, the second saying modifies such an interpretation. The rabbis here encourage young minds to begin their education immediately, not to wait until old age. A young, inquiring mind, therefore, needs to seek a mature, seasoned teacher who possesses the wisdom of the ages. The sayings end with a challenge to elderly teachers and young disciples to fill themselves with seasoned wisdom.

The full impact of the series of sayings supports social structures that call for younger disciples to submit themselves to older teachers. At the same time, however, the final statement attributed to the Rabbi (Judah) reminds all that old age does not produce automatically seasoned wisdom. Instead, it implies that wisdom in old age comes as a result of a lifelong search for knowledge. In this sense the passage challenges the elderly to grow as teachers and supports this goal by creating an environment of respect for those who pursue it.

Rabbinical sayings base respect for the elderly on beliefs about the creation of humanity. One person is worth the total of creation (ARN:31). Rabbi Akiva teaches: "Beloved is a person who was created in the image (Of God). (Still greater was the love in that it was made known directly that such was made in the image.) As it is said: 'In the divine image, God made humanity' " (Avoth 3:19).[30] According to Avoth, an elder and child equally reflect the divine image with all its potential for growth in accordance with the extravagance of God's love.

Rabbis also teach that old age comes as a reward for the righteous.

Beauty and strength and riches and honor and wisdom and old age and gray hairs and children are comely to the righteous and comely to the world. (Avoth 6:8)

In this way the Mishnah exalts old age as an additional sign of success earned by the righteous. Certainly this passage confirms the belief that old age indicates God's blessing as a fitting reward for a life well lived.

On the other hand, the Mishnah also notes the disadvantages of growing old. In the list of ages and their characteristics (Avoth 5:27), the materials describe the miseries of the ninth and tenth decades of life. Realistically, additional passages remind all that most elderly make better teachers than students (Avoth 4:25–27). Such teachings thereby balance the optimism of passages that support the leadership of the elders and remind all that frail elderly often depend on godly justice for survival.

Talmud

Talmudic collections teach more about honoring parents (kibbud 'av ve 'aim) than do sayings in the Mishnah. In a compendium of religious laws and wise sayings, rabbinical sages of Babylonia and Palestine from the third through the seventh centuries C.E. reinforce the unconditional nature of filial obligations.[31]

A renewed stress on kibbud 'av ve 'aim may indicate a developing concern in Judaism over neglect of filial responsibilities in its broadening social contexts. A restatement of the unconditional nature of filial obligations would especially address the challenges of an expanding religion which now is scattered among Gentiles. These statements thereby reinforce social structures that seem threatened anew by different cultural and religious ideas.

Talmudic rabbis teach filial reverence and illustrate these laws with examples of extreme filial obedience or mora'. An Ashkelonite Gentile is pointed out by R. Eliezer as a good example of kibbud 'av ve 'aim. Dama ben Netinah would not sell jewels for a priestly ephod at sixty thousand because the key to the jewel box is under his sleeping father's head (Kiddushin 31a). In one version of the story, sages offer him a much higher price than the jewels are worth, thinking it would induce him to sell. Dama refuses, saying he wants no payment for filial duty (Deuteronomy Rabbah).[32]

Dama again is seated among the great people of Rome, dressed in a gold garment made from silk, when his mother approaches and tears off his garment, slaps him on the head, and spits in his face—but he will not shame her (Kiddushin 31a). In another version, she hits him with a slipper. When the slipper falls from her hand, Dama picks it up and hands it to her so she would not have to bend down for it.[33] Deuteronomy Rabbah adds that his mother was mentally ill and that Dama's only reply to her public insults invariably was: "Enough, mother."[34]

Another example of self-control is also presented by R. Eliezer: "They asked R. Eliezer, 'How far must one go in *kibbud 'av ve 'aim?*' He said, 'Til the father throws the wallet of the son into the sea, and his son does not shame him.' "[35] That removes all limits for honoring parents. The parent does not need to earn the respect of offspring; rather, on the basis of being a parent, honor and reverence should be forthcoming.

Parental honor in Judaism generally takes the form of service. For example, consider the ways of Rabbi Tarfon:

> His mother went down to walk in the courtyard of the house on the Sabbath and her shoe slipped off. So he placed his hands beneath her soles and she walked on them until she reached her bed. Once he was ill and the Sages came to visit him. She said to them, "Pray on behalf of my son Tarfon, who treats me with more honor than is due to me." They asked what he had done, and she related the incident to them. They then exclaimed, "Even if he had performed a thousand times as much, he would still not have fulfilled half of what the Torah commands in connection with the honoring of parents. (P. Pe'ah 1:1; 15c)

> R. Abbahu said, "My son Abimi has fulfilled the percept of honor." Abimi had five ordained sons in his father's lifetime, yet when R. Abbahu came and called out at the door, he himself speedily went and opened it for him, crying, 'Yes, yes,' until he reached it. One day he asked him, 'Give me a drink of water.' By the time he brought it he had fallen asleep. Thereupon he bent and stood over him until he awoke. (Kiddushin 31b)[36]

Such service describes care for an aged parent by an adult child whose sense of duty to parents communicates a marvelous sense of worth and dignity. The rest of rabbinical teachings also reinforce unconditional respect and obedience for parents.

Midrash

The term Midrash indicates a body of talmudic interpretations or homilies on the Bible known as the *Haggadah*.[37] Teachers of the *Haggadah* extoll biblical characters as models of filial service. Naftali (Numbers Rabbah 14:11), Rueben (Genesis Rabbah 30:14; Genesis

Rabbah 72:2), Esau (Genesis Rabbah 65:15), and Joseph (Genesis Rabbah 84:13) all are praised for their sensitivity to the needs of their parents and for the service given to them.[38] About Joseph it is stated:

> Rabbi Tanhum in the name of R. Berekhia said, "He behaved toward him (Israel) with the proper honor, as befits the reverential obligations of a son toward a father. (Genesis Rabbah 84:13, a)

In this sense midrashic exposition reinforces common rabbinical axioms of filial respect and unconditional obedience of aging parents.

Despite differences of opinion, tannaitic admonitions generally equate honoring parents with honoring God. Later exegesis of the talmudic sources and the Bible demonstrates the continuing support in the Jewish ethos for filial reverence and honor. Respect for aging parents thereby becomes the basis for unconditional support of the leadership of the older generation and the social structure they represent.

Conclusion

Halakhot in early rabbinical literature illustrated how honoring the older generation, especially mother and father, remained an important ingredient of Jewish beliefs and practices.[39] Rabbis commanded children of all ages to honor parents unconditionally. Unlike the stress on "parental power" in Roman *patria potestas* or "parental authority" in authoritarian circles, Jewish law framed its admonitions in terms of responsibility. In Judaism children were not submitting to parental rights or demands as much as they were voluntarily giving status and service to parents. In this sense early rabbinical teachings reinforced elements of the common theology of aging which supports the status of the elderly in their social system and at the same time added their unique touch to it.

Two biblical terms remained important for Judaism: *kibbud,* "honor" and *mora',* "reverence." *Mora'* described a filial respect that demanded that a son not sit in his father's place, speak before him, or even contradict him. Father and mother were treated as superiors at all times. *Kibbud* required a son to act as the body servant of a parent and to attend to a parent's needs without thought of reward. These two terms became the basis on which the younger generation gave status and service to their elders.

The absolutization of filial respect and service in *halakhot* extended earlier biblical concepts of aging to their logical conclusions. They taught that elders (rabbis) represented divine wisdom and parents created children in partnership with God. The combination of these factors insured an exalted status for parents that extended into old age. Thereby the fear of God was equated with reverence for parents and the older person.

Literature from early Christianity and Judaism reinforced familial support for the elderly shared with Roman laws and oriental culture and at the same time modified their tenets. Christianity questioned the absolute nature of filial responsibilities where they interfered with entering the kingdom of God. When such was not an issue, Christian teachings recognized the validity of filial honor and obedience to parents and submission to the authority of older leaders. These statutes were balanced, however, by equally binding demands that fathers respect the needs of their children and not abuse parental privileges.

Rabbinical teachings, on the other hand, never questioned the wisdom of elders and the absolute nature of filial responsibilities. Children owed a debt of gratitude to parents and God, and therefore were impelled to show reverence and service to each. However, the rabbis taught that filial respect for parents, though unconditional, remained a religious duty for children. In this sense, early *halakhot* modified other emphases on parental power and authority.

In general, early Christianity and Judaism agreed on an exalted status for older persons. Respect for such persons, especially parents, was to be rendered out of religious duty in an effort to do what was right. In this way both faiths confirmed a high status for the elderly as Israel's common theology also taught. At the same time, together they made filial responsibilities more voluntary and equitable. Consequently, such teachings reinforced God's role in legitimating a just social structure that would provide stability and support for the frail and in creating an environment of respect and encouragement for leadership and growth in old age.

CHAPTER 7

Biblical Theology and
a Modern Response

An aging population offers Western religious leaders an opportunity to rediscover a heritage that may strengthen both society and the increasing numbers of the elderly. An impending aging crisis requires all to seek wisdom from a common theology of aging held by ancient oriental and subsequent cultures. At the same time, unique variations recorded in the literatures of Israel, Christianity, and Judaism have their advice to share. With this evidence biblical theology together with gerontology can confront directly social trends and mores.

Biblical theology can marshal its resources to help an aging society deal with its social turmoil. A God reported to prize justice demands that additional options be discovered for intergenerational relations. The interrelatedness of society as reflected in the people of God offers current generations a structure for mutual respect and security. Insights from the Bible may relieve members of society of the burden of misconceptions about the elderly and may allow them to replace that with positive expectations for aging.

BIBLICAL THEOLOGY AND STEREOTYPES

Overcoming the fears of growing old may rate as a priority for dealing with aging issues. Growing old brings few dividends. Society remains ambivalent about aging. Becoming old no longer is prized or unique. A common impression of the aging process portrays it as fading into oblivion and dying. Little wonder that people want to live to a ripe old age but no one wants to grow old.

The new experiences of aging perplex the elderly. They are growing old for the first time. Their bodies respond in different ways and with a myriad of changes. Advanced age can bring miseries and infirmities. As a result of these hardships, some aged become bitter, unpleasant characters. As persons enter the unknowns of aging they need a faith that shows compassion for their fears and clarifies the mysteries of growing old.

Unrealistic Expectations

Many elderly may feel pressured by the exceptional lives and health of some glorified leaders in the Bible. Moses, Caleb, Abraham, and others appear to enjoy good health until their death at a ripe old age. Bible interpretation that makes the health of outstanding persons the norm for the aging process creates ambiguity for elderly who suffer ill health. A more balanced approach, however, takes into account the many heroes in the Bible who suffered infirmities common to aging.

Isaac and Jacob experience blindness in old age (Gen. 27:1–2; 48:10). Isaac trembles when angry as if handicapped by palsy or some nervous disorder (Gen. 27:33). Moses shows anger in his grief over the death of his sister and sins (Num. 20:10–12). Eli, a priest in Shilo, is overweight, blind, and dies of a broken neck falling from his seat by the gate (1 Sam. 3:12–18). David becomes a weak, ineffective father and king in his old age (2 Samuel 11—I Kings 2:10). Solomon is said to lose his religious moorings as he ages (1 Kings 11). Paul suffers from some thorn in the flesh though it may not result from old age.

The Bible frankly describes infirmities in its heroes which often intensify with old age. Even the breakdown of a body in death is pictured with some candor (Eccles. 12:2–8). Aging adults need not condemn bodily limitations as a sign of unfaithfulness or divine disfavor. The Bible teaches that honorable elders regularly experience an aging process with its resultant health problems. Biblical theology can shift an elder's sense of worth away from unrealistic expectations for their health to a more balanced understanding of the aging process.

Fears of Inadequacy

While all need to recognize that the aging process inevitably affects their health, they need not worry that such infirmities generally lead to chronic brain disease or total physical inadequacy. Elderly leaders in the Bible contradict this misconception. They demonstrate that an aging body does not automatically stop thinking or performing at an acceptable level. No longer should a person excuse his or her poor memory on the grounds of age. Medical studies and statistics within the elderly population indicate that healthy aging adults can remain rather self-sufficient.

First of all, biblical examples refute popular misconceptions about the sexual prowess or interest of the elderly. Some believe that an older man cannot successfully perform in intercourse; others accept the misconception that elderly show little interest in intimacy. Those who do are "dirty old men" (people). The Bible demonstrates the falsity of these stereotypes.

In the Bible Sarah and Abraham reverse their own pessimism (Gen. 18:12) and produce a son. Lot overcomes the concern of his daughters and performs sexually while drunk (Gen. 19:31–38). David obliterates what remains of the misconception. Only a terminal illness can keep him from being a good lover (1 Kings 1:1–4). Aging Zechariah and Elizabeth produce a son—John (Luke 1:57–79). Only a passage in the First Epistle to Timothy comes dangerously close to expressing the false stereotype. It states that sexual desires could overcome young widows (only?) and cause them to remarry (1 Tim. 5:11–12). Yet interpreters should regard this statement as a general observation as to what regularly occurs. In that context the observation certainly is descriptive but not prescriptive of what may happen. Such an understanding of this text allows it to fit better into a nonageism model of the Bible and the common theology of the ancient Near East which recognizes that sexuality may be an important part of life at any age.

A second stereotype that biblical theology may reverse is the concept that growing old leads to some brain disease such as senile dementia or Alzheimer's disease. Evidence from ancient cultures refutes this view. Elders generally represent divine wisdom in early literatures. For example, Jacob becomes blind and somewhat dependent in his old age but still retains a clear mind (Gen. 48:19). Jethro, the father-in-law of Moses, teaches Moses a better way to judge his people (Exodus 18). Barzillai, an eighty-year-old man, provides supplies that save David at Mahanaim when he flees from Absalom

(2 Sam. 19:31–40). He remains sharp enough to be a prized asset in the court of David though he declines David's generous offer. Famous rabbis are praised for their long lives and remain alert and wise. Though it can be assumed that some elderly in the ancient world suffered from chronic brain disease, examples in the Bible and other literatures do not associate old age with it.

Instead, the Bible often describes old age as a creative time of life. Psalms 71 and 90 reflect the concerns and insights of the aging. Ecclesiastes and the Second and Third letters of John express the viewpoint of one who looks back on life and evaluates the past. Other biblical materials may also reflect the work of elderly persons (e.g., 1 Pet. 5:1; Phil. 2:22; 3:15, 16; 4:14–19). The identification of wisdom with eldership in both Judaism and Christianity finally counteracts the negative stereotype. The Bible and its related literature teach that aging may increase one's potential contribution to others and to God's work. Advanced years free the body from the restraints of hard labor and a demanding calendar. The mind thereby may be allowed to soar and focus on truth given the perspective of the mystery of death.

BIBLICAL THEOLOGY AFFIRMS SOCIAL SUPPORT

Elderly in all cultures and generations face similar problems. Elderly parents in ancient Babylon hope to salvage their security for their final years behind severe legal threats and penalties. Social laws and severe penalties protect parents from disobedient children. Destitute elderly in times of unrest and turmoil face a dismal prospect with advancing years. Aging women and widows universally are vulnerable.

Even in Israel the extended family does not eliminate isolation and loneliness from the prospects of the aging (e.g., Ps. 71:9–11). Jacob takes advantage of his nearly blind father (Genesis 27). When a person becomes sick and impoverished, society rejects that person as "unclean" (Job 30).

Problems of the elderly continue to appear in early Christian communities. The first crisis for the early church comes when Hellenistic widows are neglected (Acts 6:1–6). Disrespect for elderly leaders and neglect of the needs of widows ignite strong reactions against such behavior (1 Tim. 5:1–4, 8, 16). Judaism also relates many examples of extreme filial devotion to guard against maltreatment of aging parents. No society should be idealized as the perfect cultural pattern for solving the dilemmas of aging.

On the other hand, biblical theology provides some goals and principles which may act as useful antidotes to modern attitudes and trends. While culture in general disdains those who are financially unproductive, God acts as their protector (Lev. 19:32). The rights of widows and handicapped God supports with great passion (Exod. 22:20–23; Lev. 19:14). God's identification with the plight of the helpless in society needs to become the theologial cornerstone for treatment of modern elderly.

Family Support

Aging adults pose several severe challenges for the family. They possess approximately only 10 percent of the immunity capacity of the adolescent. Feelings of depression often accompany their loss of earlier productivity. Some feel helpless and turn their feelings of aggression on others or self. They often think they lack meaning and purpose when their role and status change. Adult pride which is important to them compounds their emotions. Some become bitter and may be hard to control. Since the nuclear family in many parts of the Western world has replaced the extended one, the problems are now compounded. Modern families are willing to help but often are unable to absorb the demands of long-term care. Care for elderly, therefore, generally is shifting to government programs or nursing homes.

Government programs and institutional care offer mixed rewards. Most elderly prefer to live independently on pensions, investments, and government retirement supplements. Only 5 percent of the elderly are under the care of a nursing home at any one time. However, institutional care or retirement pensions do not meet the emotional needs of the aging. Though nursing homes enrich and prolong the final years of many, they do not replace attention and support of family members. No matter how much nursing homes and retirement villages improve their care plans, families need to supplement that care with love and attention.

Granting dignity and respect to parents is admonished in the Ten Commandments as the foundation for family social support (Exod.

20:12). This foundational command also implies allowing independence for a parent when that is needed and supplementing an income that becomes insufficient. Jesus directly emphasizes the absolute nature of this command when he criticizes the Pharisees who abuse religious vows to escape care for their parents. Disobedience against this command characterizes degenerate people in the last times (2 Tim. 3:2; Mic. 7:6).

Admonitions from rabbinical literature to practice *mora'* and *kibbud* give additional insights into filial responsibilities. Unconditional honoring of parents is exemplified best by service. Increasing physical maladies and dependence in old age make obedience and respect mandatory for adult children. The literature of Judaism demonstrates the close relationship between God and the elderly for it equates the honoring of God with attributing worth to aging parents.

Pastoral letters imply that some Christians may have tried to evade filial demands by making the church responsible for the care of widows and aging relatives (1 Tim. 5:8, 16). Yet these biblical epistles respond that nothing replaces the family as the primary social support agency. In governmental and population crises such as the aging of the country, the family again may need to assume more direct support of the elderly. This support must be financial and emotional if the elderly are to keep some sense of self-esteem and function in a happier and more productive manner.

Weakening family ties in the present day are stripping the elderly of their best social support. Mobility especially is placing great stress on nuclear families. One conscientious family member may find herself or himself bearing the entire burden of aging parents when he or she is the only one living nearby. Christianity and Judaism both need to reemphasize their traditions of family interdependence. Only within a caring family may an aging adult receive respect without regard to health, beauty, sex, or economic independence. Society may not return to an extended family structure but still needs to achieve some of its goals. The common theology of aging in the Bible, both shared and unique, can help family members treat one another with respect, especially honoring the aging ones.

Productive Roles for the Elderly

Retirement in Western cultures means something far different from what it signifies in the ancient Eastern world. Though changes occur in the roles of the elderly in ancient cultures, no mandatory ceasing of productive labor is implied. In the Western world an older person feels compelled to exit from leadership and profitable endeavors. Only in exceptional cases where one owns a business and continues as an entrepreneur will that not happen. Otherwise a business tells retirees they no longer are profitable to either self or society. Compare this attitude with insights from biblical practice and expectations.

Biblical leadership is synonymous with eldership. This expectation commonly appears in the literature of ancient cultures. Elders judge local disputes and act as family, tribal, synagogue, and church leaders. Maturity, although not always a product of old age in the modern sense of the term, remains the primary qualification. Elders are ones who possess the wisdom and experience for making important decisions for the welfare of all.

Role transitions within Western culture need redefining and reflection. When aging is associated with idleness and privation, tensions intensify between the elderly and the young. The young may treat the retired as scapegoats when government spending and taxes soar to finance their retirement plans. Elderly citizens feel threatened when rising health care costs tax their financial resources at the same time their pensions are limited. When older employees work full time, some criticize them for occupying positions needed by younger employees or the unemployed. Intergenerational struggles result.

Scheduling life transitions through which leadership and employment can be shared by all generations remains a major challenge for Western society. Business, religion, and the community cannot afford to ignore such structural ambiguity. Only the aggressive, powerful, and rich benefit from the present system. Families must begin to honor their patriarchs and matriarchs as leaders. Such an attitude needs to carry over into churches, synagogues, and community organizations.

Instead of merely developing programs to keep the elderly occupied (off the street?), churches and synagogues need to utilize the experience and wisdom of these leaders in realistic ways. Organizations can develop programs of enrichment and provide opportunities for travel and education. At the same time, however, religious groups should seek the advice of, and employ in reasonable ways, their retired leaders. Neither life nor leadership ends at age sixty-five. Rather, a respectful attitude and responsive transition structures may enhance both.

Self-Esteem for Elderly

Competition between the generations is not new. Clashes over inheritance rights dominate generational concerns in ancient literatures. However, the value many Western cultures place on competition heightens recent intergenerational dilemmas. A revival of a theory of scarcity in light of limited energy and food resources is raising conflict to new levels. Consequently, generations clash over energy demands as opposed to conservation, over an adequate education as opposed to increased property taxes, over increased social security taxes as opposed to benefit increases.

Clashes between the needs of elderly and those of younger adults could ease if both generations felt themselves recognized and heard. Satisfaction of mutual concerns for self-esteem would ease the sense of competition which emotional responses complicate. Biblical theology can provide a basis for eliminating so-called ageism.

Self-esteem for the elderly would increase considerably when all recognize the privilege of growing older. Youth could appreciate in a new way aging hair and faces (Lev. 19:32). Truly, society might recognize that white hair is an achievement, a "crown of glory" (Prov. 16:31). White hair and the postmature body might once again represent experience and precious resources. Honored elders would not be excluded from life or social support. Christians would not confuse old age with the polemic of the Synoptic Gospels against enemy "elders," "traditions of the elders," or what they consider old, obsolete practices. The "new ways," "new life," and "new age" would not exclude older adults (2 Cor. 4:16). Aging adults would not be identified with the "old person" of sin, death, and immorality. Preparing messages speaking of old age as a blessing of God would do much to increase the self-esteem of the elderly.

A modern throw-away society does not need to be persuaded that old is useless and only the new has value. Old buildings, cars, computers, and appliances daily are disposed of in that culture. Only the new improved versions appear precious or marketable. Unfortunately, modern Western societies evaluate persons by the same standards, abusing passages such as: "New wine cannot be put in old wineskins" (Mark 7:3). As growing old becomes more commonplace, its esteem is decreasing. Society needs to make plans to include the elderly in its hierarchy of values. Modern persons need to recognize that potential newness rests in any individual.

BIBLICAL THEOLOGY CHALLENGES THE ELDERLY TO GROW

Despite ageism in Western society and its oppressive structures, older adults themselves determine their future happiness. On the one hand, they can allow others to chart their future and to set their self-esteem and then blame the younger generation for their terrible plight. That alternative feeds on passivity and leads to bitterness. On the other hand, senior adults may recognize that to some degree their future comes out of their own efforts. They indeed shape their personal attitudes and destiny. Biblical theology encourages the activist approach through what it teaches about the nature of people and the blessings of God.

To Grow as the Image of God

Unfortunately, Western societies generally idolize youth as the apex of human development. Advertising and media programming glamorize youthfulness. The ideal model is young, robust, daring, strong, beautiful or handsome, and affluent. Churches seek leaders who model this youthfulness. After thirty, life declines drastically. In practice society excludes the elderly from the image of God.

To correct an overemphasis on youthfulness as the primary factor in beauty and worth, modern Christianity needs to reexamine its theological roots. These theological moorings begin with the creation of male and female in the image of God (Gen. 1:27). Recently, Christians are recognizing that this image includes both sexes. As well, a number remind society that children reflect that image. New advocates need to arise to remind the elderly and the young that the wrinkling of skin and graying of hair do not diminish the image of God within a person.

Persons moving toward and beyond age sixty-five need assurance that the likeness of God knows no age limitations. They need reminding that every age group possesses adequate potential for creativity and spiritual rejuvenation. Youth remains only a brief span of life (Eccles. 11:9—12:2; Ps. 90:12). Though aging brings some physical changes, meaningful service and happiness can continue.

Such a message needs to penetrate the health care industry. Medical schools only peripherally prepare their graduates for dealing with the complex physical and mental problems of aging. Too often medical personnel associate aging with death and therefore may find it difficult to provide adequate medical care for the chronic conditions of the elderly. New respect for the image of God which all reflect may help key persons overcome the stigma that the possibility of death attaches. Biblical theology teaches that aging adults also carry with them life and potential health.

Middle-aged adults moving toward old age also long for assurance that life does not end at sixty-five. Persons struggling with a sense of mortality through the middle years welcome words of encouragement from the over-sixty generation. Expectancy and optimism hopefully might replace their gnawing anxiety about aging and dying. Realizing that the image of God prepares all to live fruitfully in each transition of life may enable anyone to enjoy each moment of life as it occurs.

A theology of personhood needs to include the elderly in its dialogue. Properly understood, it may grant dignity to those whose status and health might appear to be worsening. As replicas of God the elderly retain their value as persons whose contributions to all generations should not be ignored. This broadened theology of personhood need not neglect the young; rather, it hopefully will balance the values of a youth-oriented society and religious communities.

To Grow as Lifelong Learners

Wisdom does not arrive for anyone automatically when hair turns to silver. A biblical theology of personhood points out that an understanding mind develops out of a lifelong struggle for knowledge. Wisdom literature especially emphasizes this fact. As older friends frustrated Job and Elihu with simple answers (Job 12:12–13; 32:6–9), so elderly who live content with superficial answers may short-circuit their wisdom potential.

Biblical examples challenge all to move beyond superficiality to become lifelong learners. Jethro, the father-in-law of Moses, Moses himself, Joshua, Caleb, Barzillai, the older counselors of Rehoboam,

Simeon, Anna, and early Jewish rabbis represent the best in lifelong learning. Lessons from these examples, undergirded by a high view of the potential of God's greatest creation, present a demanding challenge for growth to the older generation.

Common foolishness also found in the elderly stresses the need to work at becoming a lifelong learner. In the Bible an old prophet tricks a young one from Judah and costs the young prophet his life (1 Kings 13:11–32). Palestinian elders in the Synoptic Gospels reject the innovative message of the kingdom. Even an older religious leader named Nicodemus seems perplexed when asked to change in his old age (John 3:4). Biblical theology does not assume that a person achieves wisdom by aging even though the potential may be present as a result of the blessings of God.

Though true wisdom comes from God, it never arrives automatically, as Ben Sira and the Book of Wisdom point out. It must be grasped by learning the lessons of life through discipline and obedience (Prov. 1:7–8; 6:23). Elderly learners first of all must put aside misconceptions that people grow too old to learn. Instead, they need to dedicate themselves to personal discipline through which they may acquire the wisdom of the ages. Such is the key to becoming a lifelong learner.

CONCLUSION

Aging is never without its problems. Biblical theology, however, can ease some of its mystery. Biblical teaching can promote realistic yet positive expectations to alleviate some burdens of ageism. Through its insights about the blessings of God it relieves ambivalence about growing old.

Because of biblical examples, physical expectations become less of a burden and more of a challenge to growth. They shatter stereotypes and help us appreciate and utilize the ultimate value and potential of the elderly. A mutually supportive family reinforces social support for the old, and lessens aging fears. In light of the Bible, old age will not rule out leadership and transitions may occur in an equitable manner. All this hinges on whether persons hear and encounter the intent and message of the God who provides supportive structures for the frail.

In any case, the relationship between God and the elderly remains secure. Divine concern for their plight and utilization of their potential does not change. Both the common and unique aspects of Israel's heritage on aging reinforce that. As God delivers Israel in its transitions, so God cares for the aging.

> To your old age I am the one (who will look after you); to gray hair I will carry (you). I myself have created (you) and will lift you up; I myself will carry and deliver (you).
>
> (Isa. 46:4)

Though others abandon the aging, God will not cast them away.

Abbreviations

ANET	*Ancient Near Eastern Texts*
ARM	Archives royales de Mari
BA	*Biblical Archaeologist*
BDB	Brown, Driver, Briggs, *Hebrew and English Lexicon of the Old Testament*
BZAW	Beihefte zur *ZAW*
CAD	*Assyrian Dictionary of the Oriental Institute of the University of Chicago*
CBQ	Catholic Biblical Quarterly
CTA	*Corpus des tablettes en cunéiformes alphabétiques découvertes à Ras Shamra-Ugarit de 1929 à 1939*
HUCA	*Hebrew Union College Annual*
IDB	*Interpreter's Dictionary of the Bible*
IEJ	*Israel Exploration Journal*
JBL	*Journal of Biblical Literature*
JNES	*Journal of Near Eastern Studies*
JTS	*Journal of Theological Studies*
KB	Kohler, Baumgartner, *Lexicon in Veteris Testamenti libros*
NICOT	New International Commentary of the Old Testament
TDOT	*Theological Dictionary of the Old Testament,* ed. G. J. Botterweek and H. Ringgren
UT	*Ugaritic Textbook*
ZAW	*Zeitschrift für die alttestamentliche Wissenschaft*

Notes

INTRODUCTION

1. David O. Moberg, who studied the personal adjustment of the aged in institutions, concluded that the better adjusted were more active in "religion," "believers" rather than "nonbelievers" ("Religion and Personal Adjustment in Old Age" [diss., Univ. of Minnesota, 1951]). For an annotated bibliography in this area, see Vincent John Fecher, *Religion and Aging: An Annotated Bibliography* (San Antonio: Trinity Univ. Press, 1982), 23–26.

2. The implications of this population shift, with a full breakdown of the statistics, may be explored fully in Charles S. Harris, *Fact Book on Aging: A Profile of America's Older Population* (Washington, D.C.: National Council on Aging, 1978–79). Statistics are compiled from the 1980 census in a popular form within the tract "A Profile of Older Americans" (Washington, D.C.: American Association of Retired Persons, 1984).

3. Economic aspects of this change are discussed by Juanita M. Kreps in "Human Values, Economic Values, and the Elderly," in *Aging, Death, and the Completion of Being*, ed. David D. Van Tassel (Philadelphia: Univ. of Pennsylvania Press, 1979), 20–26; additional discussion can be found in a series of papers prepared by Juanita Kreps, Joseph J. Spengler, R. Stanley Herren, and Robert Clark for the National Science Foundation, *The Economics of a Stationary Population: Implications for the Elderly* (Washington, D.C.: National Science Foundation, 1975).

4. See the demographic data concerning European and other countries culled from the United Nations' 1975 demographic yearbook by Edman Palmone, in *International Handbook on Aging*, ed. Edman Palmone (Westport, Conn.: Greenwood Press, 1980), xix. For Germany, see Hans Peter Bleuel, *Alte Menschen in Deutschland* (Munich: Carl Hanser Verlag, 1972), 13–15.

5. For extensive discussion on the issues of long-term-care costs and services, see John Hendricks and C. David Hendricks, *Aging in Mass Society:*

Myths and Realities, 2d ed. (Cambridge, Mass.: Winthrop Pubs., 1981), 221–33; *Summary of the 1985 Federal and State Legislative Policy of the American Association of Retired Persons,* 17–29; and Charlene Harrington et al., *Long Term Care of the Elderly,* Sage Library of Social Research 157 (Beverly Hills, Calif.: Sage Pubs., 1985), 251–69.

6. See Claus Westermann, *Blessing in the Bible and the Life of the Church,* trans. Keith Crim, Overtures to Biblical Theology (Philadelphia: Fortress Press, 1978), 4–5.

7. So argues K. Brynolf Lyon in *Toward a Practical Theology of Aging,* Theology and Pastoral Care (Philadelphia: Fortress Press, 1986), 109–19. The trivialization of age in the current context and the chronic conditions associated with an increasing age span make it important to reconceptualize old age as a blessing in the above categories.

8. For thorough discussions of the significance of blessing in the Bible, see Johannes Pedersen, *Israel: Its Life and Culture,* 2 vols. (London: Oxford Univ. Press, 1926), 1:182–212; and Westermann, *Blessing in the Bible,* 27–101.

9. See Walter Brueggemann, "A Shape for Old Testament Theology, II," *CBQ* 47 (1985): 398ff. Brueggemann identifies this ideology as "common theology" and contrasts it with the "pain embrace" resulting from "any dysfunction in the relationship with God" or any "disorder of creation or society," as evidenced clearly in the laments.

10. The guidelines addressed are outlined and discussed in more detail in Robert R. Wilson's *Prophecy and Society in Ancient Israel* (Philadelphia: Fortress Press, 1980), 14–19; and in his *Sociological Approaches to the Old Testament,* Guides to Biblical Scholarship (Philadelphia: Fortress Press, 1984), 26–29.

11. See David Maldonaldo, "Towards a Theology of Aging in the Christian Community" (Unpub. ms. delivered at NICA, Washington, D.C., November 11-13, 1985), 2ff.

12. E.g., Carol LeFevre and Perry LeFevre, eds., *Aging and the Human Spirit* (Chicago: Exploration Press, 1981), esp. 1–3; and Francis V. Tiso, ed., *Aging: Spiritual Perspectives* (Lake Worth, Fla.: Sunday Pubs., 1982), esp. the article by Asher Finkel, "Aging: The Jewish Perspective," 113.

13. See Walter Brueggemann, "A Shape for Old Testament Theology, I: Structure Legitimation," *CBQ* 47 (1985): 31–34. Brueggemann illustrates the method in discussing laments, in "A Shape for Old Testament Theology, II."

14. In deference to the concern of Judaism, the divine tetragrammaton normally will be translated "Lord" or "Adonai."

CHAPTER 1.   AGING EXPERIENCES AND
THE BIBLE

1. Earlier work on the life span in this era can be found in Lorenz Durr's *Die Wertung des Lebens im Alten Testament und im antiken Orient* (Münster, 1926) and in the more recent articles of Josef Scharbert ("Das Alter und die

Alten in der Bibel," *Saeculum* 30 [1979]: 338–54) and Johann Maier ("Die Wertung des Alters in der judischen Überlieferung der Spatantike und des frühen Mittelalters," *Saeculum* 30 [1979]: 355–64).

2. Akkadian uses a number of words to describe the various age groups: 40 years, *la-tu-tu*, "prime of life" (*CAD* 9:52); 50 years, *umu-ar-ku-tu*, "short life"; 60 years, *ši-pa-tu*, "wool"; and 90 years, *lit-tu-tu*, "extreme old age" (*CAD* 9:220–21). The word *ši-pa-tu*, meaning "wool," as well as *ši-bu*, is used for *alt, alter, Greis Altester* and *grauhaarig*. Cf. Wolfram von Soden in *Akkadisches Handwörterbuch* (Wiesbaden: Otto Harrassowitz, 1981), 3:1228, 1244. Hebrew uses the cognate word *shevah*, "gray head," as a synonym for old age (BDB, 966 s.v.): Gen. 15:5; 25:8; Judges 8:32; 1 Chron. 29:28; Rev. 4:15.

3. The Hebrew word *zaqen*, and its equivalents *sibtum* (in Akkadian), *senator* (in Latin), *gerōn* (in Greek), and *shekh* (in Arabic), designate both people of advanced age and people of a distinct social grade. The Hebrew word derives from the word for one who wears a beard *(zaqan)*, i.e., a fully accredited adult. See KB, and also BDB, s.v. *zaqen*. For discussions of the elders as constituting a distinct social grade or position, see G. Bornkamm in *Theological Word Book of the New Testament* 6:40, 522, 540; and A. E. Harvey, "Elders," *JTS* n.s. 25 (1974): 318–32.

4. The following Hebrew idioms appear in the Bible: *'orek yamin*, "length of days"; *yamim rabbim*, "many days"; *s'ba'yamim*, "sated with days"; *m'le'yamim*, "full of days"; *ba'bayyim*, "advanced in years"; and *sebah tobah*, "a ripe old age." Verbal forms include *ha'arek yamim*, "to lengthen days"; *harbot yamim*, "to increase days"; and *hosep yamin*, "to add days." A. Malamat ("Longevity: Biblical Concepts and Some Ancient Near Eastern Parallels," *Archiv für Orientforschung* 19 [1982]: 215) mentions that the expression *'rk ymm ('orek yamim?)* was discovered in a Hebrew inscription at Kuntillet ʿAjrud, dating from the late 9th to early 8th cent. B.C.E. He also notes other counterparts of the above phrases found in West Semitic languages and in Akkadian.

5. The aging experience and its nuances in the Hebrew Scriptures are discussed by Jean-Pierre Prevost in "Vieiller ou pas vieiller? Le point de vue de l'Ancien Testament," *Eglise et Théologie* 16 (1985): 9-23. Though incomplete, the view of aging in the Old Testament has much to recommend it.

6. See Hans Walter Wolff, *Anthropology of the Old Testament*, trans. Margaret Kohl (London: SCM Press, 1974), 119–23; and Johannes Pedersen, *Israel: Its Life and Culture*, 2 vols. (London: Oxford Univ. Press, 1926), 2:46. Wolff employs the chronology of Alfred Jepsen and R. Hanhart (*Untersuchungen zur israelitisch—jüdischen Chronologie*, BZAW 88 [1964]) in comparing the lives of the fourteen kings. Supplemental chronological data from Greek recensions are presented by James Donald Shenkel (*Chronology and Recensional Development to the Greek Text of Kings*, Harvard Semitic Monographs 1 [Cambridge: Harvard Univ. Press, 1968], 22-42). He prefers the Old

Greek chronology over that of the MT (pp. 109–11). But variations in regnal chronology do not change the basic conclusion given above.

7. Perhaps the three 40-year stages of Moses' life reflect those three seasons of life. As well, the 40-year reigns of Saul, David, and Solomon may refer to the fulfilling of the final maturity/elderly season. Malamat ("Longevity," 216–18) notes that the Bible defines a maximum life span as one enduring to the fourth generation of a family. This he then equates with the life span of 70 to 80 years mentioned in Ps. 90:10. Still, not many elderly lived to age 70 or 80 and four generations in one household must also have been rare.

8. The beginning age may have fluctuated during the history of Israel or may have differed with the branch of priesthood, the kingdom, or the geographical area. The initial age is lowered to 20 years and there is no retirement age in 1 Chron. 23:24. Cf. R. Abba, "Priests and Levites," in *IDB* 3:880. For additional information on the Kohathite Levites, see Aelred Cody, *A History of the Priesthood,* Analecta Biblica 35 (Rome: Pontifical Biblical Institute, 1969), 172–73.

9. Chapter 27 appears to be some sort of P appendix added to the so-called Holiness Code (Leviticus [17], 18—26). For discussion of the H source, see J. Milgram, "Leviticus," in *IDBSup,* 543–45. In this chapter dealing with vows, the key word is "evaluation," *'ere-ke-ka.*

10. See G. J. Wenham, "Leviticus 27:28 and the Price of Slaves," *ZAW* 90 (1978): 264–65; idem, *The Book of Leviticus* (Grand Rapids: Wm. B. Eerdmans, 1979); Ephraim A. Speiser, *Oriental and Biblical Studies,* ed. Moshe Greenberg and Jacob J. Finkelstein (Philadelphia: Univ. of Pennsylvania Press, 1967), 124ff.; and I. Mendelsohn, *Slavery in the Ancient Near East* (New York: Oxford Univ. Press, 1949), 117ff.

11. Luke-Acts mentions that early Christians continued to care for widows, such as neglected gentile ones (Acts 6:1; 9:39). Jesus praises the widow who gave the last of her money to the temple (Luke 21:1–4) and shows special compassion for a widow whose only son died (Luke 7:11–16). He angrily denounces those who "devour widow's houses" and then pray long prayers (Luke 20:47). An epistle defines "pure religion" as the visiting of orphans and widows in their affliction (James 1:27).

CHAPTER 2. ATTITUDES TOWARD THE ELDERLY
IN THE ANCIENT NEAR EAST

1. Though the uniform texts of the so-called Babylonian Ecclesiastes date only from the 7th cent. B.C.E., the poem may be several centuries older (*ANET,* 439). A case can be made that the initial subject of this speech may be the gods, not the people as assumed by Robert F. Pfeiffer (*ANET,* 440). E.g., "The mind of the god, like the center of the heavens" (XXV.1.273–74) "is remote: His knowledge is difficult, men cannot understand it" (XXIV.264). Whether the subject is gods or the people, the lack of justice in the world makes life under the control of the gods seem very capricious.

2. Note the discussion of Mesopotamian culture and religion by Thorkild Jacobson in H. A. Frankfort et al., *The Intellectual Adventure of Ancient Man* (Chicago: Univ. of Chicago Press, 1946), 125, 202. Cf. Thorkild Jacobsen, *The Treasures of Darkness: A History of Mesopotamian Religion* (New Haven: Yale Univ. Press, 1976). Religious myths in the third millennium B.C.E. emphasized the metaphors of the gods as rulers. Second-millennium texts described the gods as parents and as the origin of world order (*Treasures of Darkness,* 77–219). The chaos of the first millennium weakened the provider metaphor, which gave way to the ruler motifs with their social and political concerns (pp. 226–32).

3. Cf. G. R. Driver and John C. Miles, *The Babylonian Laws* (Oxford: At the Clarendon Press, 1955), 2:75–77, nos. 192–93, 195.

4. Ibid., 309, nos. 1, 2. Though these law tablets are sometimes idealistic, they contain valuable information about the legal heritage of Mesopotamia.

5. Ibid., 59, no. 150.

6. Edmund I. Gordon, *Sumerian Proverbs: Glimpses of Everyday Life in Ancient Mesopotamia* (Philadelphia: University Museum, University of Pennsylvania, 1959), 197. The Sumerian proverb 2.33 comes from Nippur and is dated to the Old Babylonian period (p. 152).

7. Cf. Driver and Miles, *Babylonian Laws* 2:65, 309–11. In the latter texts, notice how parents could be punished for disinheriting a son.

8. W. G. Lambert, *Babylonian Wisdom Literature* (Oxford: At the Clarendon Press, 1960), 248 (iii, ll. 7–10).

9. Cf. ibid., 128–31 (ll. 99–100).

10. Gordon, *Sumerian Proverbs,* 114. Proverb 1.145 also appears in UM 29–15–394 iii 5–6. It comes from Nippur and is generally assigned to the first third of the second millennium B.C.E., though it could reflect a considerably earlier date.

11. For additional information on the subject, see Rainer Albertz, "Hintergrund und Bedeutung des Elterngebots im Dekalog," *ZAW* 90 (1978): 356–64.

12. Gordon, *Sumerian Proverbs,* 110. This proverb expresses a familiar theme: He/she bites off his/her nose to spite his/her face! The Sumerian proverb 1.141 also dates from the first third of the second millennium B.C.E.

13. Cf. John A. Wilson, "Egypt: The Values of Life," in Frankfort et al., *The Intellectual Adventure of Ancient Man,* 93–118; and William W. Hallo and William Kelly Simpson, "Egypt," in *The Ancient Near East: A History* (New York: Harcourt Brace Jovanovich, 1971), 234–41.

14. Note "The Instruction of the Visier Ptah-hotep" (*ANET,* 412ff.), where the author describes the disabilities of old age in very realistic terms and then the older person asks that his son might listen to the "ideas of the ancestors," to those who "hearkened to the gods" (ll. 30–31).

15. See Miriam Lichtheim, *Ancient Egyptian Literature,* vol. 2, *The New*

Kingdom (Berkeley and Los Angeles: Univ. of California Press, 1976), 135–46.

16. Though MS. copies date from a later period, composition of "The Instruction of Amen-em-ophet" normally is accepted as having occurred in the Ramesside period (ibid., 146–63). Cf. discussion on this text's relationship to Proverbs in William McKane, *Proverbs: A New Approach*, Old Testament Library (Philadelphia: Westminster Press, 1970), 102–17, 371–73.

17. Demotic literature from Egypt's later period, e.g., "The Instruction of Ankhsheshonq," echoes the same level of respect for elders (Lichtheim, *New Kingdom*, 164–65, 168–70, 175).

18. For the information on the work at Ugarit, examine the essays in *Ugarit in Retrospect: Fifty Years of Ugarit and Ugaritic*, ed. Gordon D. Young (Winona Lake, Ind.: Eisenbrauns, 1981), and the articles by James M. Robinson, Peter Craigie, Claude F. A. Schaeffer in "Remembering Ugarit," *Biblical Archaeological Review* 9/5 (September–October 1983): 54–75. Additional resources are listed in "A Guide for Further Study and Reading," in P. C. Craigie's *Ugarit and the Old Testament* (Grand Rapids: Wm. B. Eerdmans, 1983), 102–10.

19. E.g., *ANET*, 129, 137–38. The poems tell of Baal's superiority over rebellious gods, esp. Yamm. Even El surrenders Baal to Yamm. Only Baal can crush the enemy. In the Baal and Anath cycle, Anath likewise evidences no respect for either older persons or gods. Cf. John Gibson, *Canaanite Myths and Legends* (Edinburgh: T. & T. Clark, 1977), 47, 54; Samuel Noah Kramer, ed., *Mythologies of the Ancient World* (Garden City, N.Y.: Doubleday & Co., 1961), 190–217; and Theodor H. Gaster, *Thespis*, rev. ed. (New York: Harper & Row, 1961), 110–24, 316–26.

20. Complex social, political, and religious pressures certainly brought about this religious revolution. Amorite invaders and the Hurrian preference for Hadad, the storm god, probably contributed to Ba'al's usurping of the throne of El. Cf. discussions by Marvin Pope (*El in the Ugaritic Texts*, Supplements to Vetus Testamentum 2 [Leiden: E. J. Brill, 1955]), A. S. Kapelrud (*Baal in Ras Shamra Texts* [Copenhagen, 1953]; *The Violent Goddess: Anat in the Ras Shamra Texts* [Oslo, 1969], esp. 110–13; and "The Relationship between Baal and El in the Ras Shamra Texts," in *Bible World: Essays in Honor of Cyrus Gordon*, ed. Gary Rendsburg et al. [New York: KTAV, 1980], 79–85), and Ulf Oldenburg (*The Conflict between El and Baal in Canaanite Religion* [Leiden: E. J. Brill, 1969], 143–63). See Giovanni Pettinato ("Pre-Ugaritic Documentation of Ba'al," in *Bible World*, ed. Rendsburg et al., 203–9), who proposes an alternate origin for Ba'al.

21. Text UT 52 (KTU 1.23, CTA 23) may predate the displacement of El as the premier deity (*Mythologies*, ed. Kramer, 185–90). Cf. John Gray, "Social Aspects of Canaanite Religion," in *Volume du Congrès Genève, 1965*, Supplements to Vetus Testamentum 15 (Leiden: E. J. Brill, 1966), 170–92; and idem, *The Canaanites* (New York: Frederick A. Praeger; London:

Thames & Hudson, 1964). The lines form the second part of a work conventionally called the Poem of the Gracious Gods, which Gaster (*Thespis,* 409–15, 427–35) terms a burlesque treatment of a myth.

22. Cf. Michael David Coogan, *Stories from Ancient Canaan* (Philadelphia: Westminster Press, 1978), 33; Gray, "Social Aspects of Canaanite Religion," 174; and idem, *The Legacy of Canaan,* Supplements to Vetus Testamentum 5 (Leiden: E. J. Brill, 1957), 185–86. Also cf. KTU 1.17 and CTB 17 i, 26–35, for the full passage; and Gibson, *Canaanite Myths,* 104.

23. Cf. John Khanjian, "Wisdom in Ugarit and in the ANE with Particular Emphasis on Old Testament Wisdom Literature" (diss., Claremont, Grad. School, 1973), 166ff. (II:7, 32). Concern for the mother appears in a father's will and testament from Ugarit (*ANETSup,* 546).

24. An epilogue in the story of Ham's insult to his father, Noah (Gen. 9:18–27), secondarily mentions Noah's curse on Canaan. Though this passage polemically explains why the Canaanites were enslaved by Israel, it indirectly associates the Canaanites with parental disrespect and violations of its ideals recorded in 2 Aqhat. Cf. Claus Westermann, *Genesis 1–11: A Commentary,* trans. John J. Scullion (Minneapolis: Augsburg Pub. House, 1984), 488–89.

25. *ANET,* 147–49; John Gray, *The KRT Text in the Literature of Ras Shamra: A Social Myth of Ancient Canaan,* 2d ed. (Leiden: E. J. Brill, 1964), 2; and Gibson, *Canaanite Myths,* 94. Cf. Coogan, *Stories,* 70–74.

26. See Khanjian, *Wisdom in Ugarit,* 122–34.

27. In 1887 an Egyptian peasant woman discovered a collection totaling some 377 cuneiform tablets in Middle Egypt at Tell-el-Amarna, the 14th-cent. B.C.E. site of the capital of Akh-en-Aton. See *ANET,* 483–90. Some three hundred of these letters appear to have been written by Canaanite scribes in Palestine (about half), Phoenicia, and southern Syria. Most date from the last years of Amen-hotep III and the reign of his successor. E.g., R. A. xix (p. 97) mentions governors and corvée labor. A number of letters mention cities, crown property, and regular tribute (*ANET,* 486–87). See also W. F. Albright, *The Amarna Letters from Palestine, Syria, the Philistines, and Phoenicia,* vol. 2 (Cambridge: At the Univ. Press, 1966), 7–20; and J. A. Knudtzon, with Otto Weber and E. Ebeling, eds., *Die El-Amarna-Tafeln mit Einleitung und Erlauterungen,* 2 vols. (Aalen: Otto Zelder, 1964).

28. Cf. A. F. Rainey, "A Canaanite at Ugarit" (UT311), *IEJ* 13 (1963): 43–45; idem, "Business Agents at Ugarit," *IEJ* 13 (1963): 313–21; and idem, "Ugarit and Canaanites Again," *IEJ* 14 (1964): 101. Though Rainey suggests that citizenry of Ugarit were a political entity separate from the Canaanites, these documents also suggest that cultural ties were maintained. For further information on the social stratification of Ras Shamra, see idem, "The Kingdom of Ugarit," *BA* 28 (1965): 102–25; idem, "Family at Ugarit," *Orientalia* 24 (1965): 10–22; and idem, "The Military Personnel of Ugarit," *JNES* 24 (1965): 17–27. The textual evidence is compiled in idem, "The Social Stratification of Ugarit" (diss., Brandeis Univ., 1962).

29. Though the system in Canaan differed somewhat from European feudalism, it included basic feudal forms—city-states, autonomous and competitive, under the domination of Egypt. See Norman K. Gottwald, *The Tribes of Yahweh: A Sociology of the Religion of Liberated Israel, 1250–1050 B.C.E.* (Maryknoll, N.Y.: Orbis Books, 1979), 392–98.

CHAPTER 3. GOD AND THE ELDERLY IN ISRAEL

1. The blow need not be a fatal one. Later Jewish interpreters limited the punishment to a striking that produced a wound or bruise. E.g., *Mekilta* de Rabbi Ismael, Rashi, and Rashbom. The LXX switches vv. 16 and 17 to tie together logically the threats in vv. 15 and 17.

2. The participial formulation *um qallel* found here is studied in detail by A. Jirku (*Das weltliche Recht* [Gutersloh, 1927]). For a study in parallels in this use of the "curse," see H. C. Brichto, *The Problem of "Curse" in the Hebrew Bible,* SBL and Exegesis JBL Monograph Series 13 (Philadelphia, 1963), 132–35. Exodus 21:12–17 contains a compilation of ancient laws against capital offenses. This series of participial clauses originally may have connected to 22:18, the only other example of the participial style in the Book of the Covenant. Cf. Brevard S. Childs, *The Book of Exodus,* Old Testament Library (Philadelphia: Westminster Press, 1974), 470.

3. Ancient people considered *'arur,* "cursed," as having real destructive power. The curse comes from God and might establish itself on a worshiper and household. Cf. G. von Rad, *Deuteronomy: A Commentary,* Old Testament Library (Philadelphia: Westminster Press, 1966), 167–69. For additional study on the history of treaty curses, see D. R. Hillers, *Treaty-Curses and Old Testament Prophets* (Rome: Pontifical Biblical Institute, 1964), 12–35. The list of twelve curses in Deut. 27:15–26 has a fixed pattern and rhythm, as does Deuteronomy 28. Such lists are formed out of a gathering and adaptation of traditional materials.

4. Cf. Peter Craigie, *The Book of Deuteronomy,* NICOT (Grand Rapids: Wm. B. Eerdmans, 1976), 331–32.

5. Verse 9 represents a problem, for *ki* seems to connect the verse to vv. 7 and 8 but in content the verse fits better with vv. 10–21. Probably the verse is quoting the statute found in its original phrasing in Exod. 21:17, and with *'arur* in Deut. 27:16. Cf. Martin Noth, *Leviticus: A Commentary* (Philadelphia: Westminster Press, 1965), 149.

6. Cf. the use of the phrase in Ezek. 18:13 and 33:5 and in this chapter as a coda to several laws (vv. 11, 12, 13, 16, 27). It has its parallel in the more common phrase "his blood be on his head" (e.g., Josh. 2:19; 2 Sam. 1:16). Cf. G. J. Wenham, *The Book of Leviticus,* NICOT (Grand Rapids: Wm. B. Eerdmans, 1979), 275–79; and Noth, *Leviticus,* 150.

7. The example fits within a chapter containing a number of legislative judgments dealing with the nature of a crime, how a crime should be tried, and its resulting punishment. Such subjects as murder, war, and family affairs

are treated in these independent passages. Most of the crimes and procedures have parallels in Near Eastern literature. Cf. Craigie, *Book of Deuteronomy,* 278. Whether such an execution actually happened or not is unknown. Nevertheless, its threat reinforces the seriousness of other statutes supporting the honoring of parents.

8. The verse calling for respect of the gray head and older face reflects a common sense of awe at the signs of old age. But the last half of the verse reflects themes commonly found in the priestly Holiness Code. The phrases reinforce the basic message of the text, though they are not integral to its basic point. A *Selbstvorstellungsformel* concludes the verse giving the holy name of the God of Israel. Such a formula of self-introduction adds to the significance of the particular command and those preceding it. For additional study, see Walther Zimmerli, *I Am Yahweh,* trans. D. W. Stott, ed. Walter Brueggemann (Atlanta: John Knox Press, 1982), 1–28.

9. E.g., Klaus Koch, *The Prophets: The Assyrian Period,* vol. 1 (Philadelphia: Fortress Press, 1982), 32; J. Lindblom, *Prophecy in Ancient Israel* (Philadelphia: Fortress Press, 1965), 202–19; and Robert R. Wilson, *Prophecy and Society in Ancient Israel* (Philadelphia: Fortress Press, 1980), 89–134.

10. See A. R. Johnson, *The Cultic Prophet in Ancient Israel* (Cardiff: Univ. of Wales Press, 1962), 14ff. Impressive parallels to Israelite prophecy have come to light in the royal archives discovered in the ruins of the ancient Amorite kingdom in Mari of Upper Mesopotamia. Cf. *ANET,* 623–32; and Joseph Blenkinsopp, *A History of Prophecy in Israel* (Philadelphia: Westminster Press, 1983), 56–59. In general the messages in Mari are supportive of the king and his political and military goals. Indications in other sites are that the Mari situation was fairly typical of Mesopotamian prophecy (e.g., ARM 10.6, 7). Tablets from Mari indicate that there were two general groups of prophets, some of whom enjoyed a prominent social position but others of whom had no title and played no definite social role (Wilson, *Prophecy and Society,* 100–110).

11. For a Near Eastern parallel with this oracle, see A. Malamat, "A Mari Prophecy and Nathan's Dynastic Oracle," in *Prophecy: Essays Presented to George Fohrer on His Sixty-fifth Birthday,* ed. J. A. Emerton (Berlin: Walter de Gruyter, 1980), 68–82. On the basis of this parallel (A. 1121) and others (e.g., A. 2731), numerous foreign influences have been pointed out in the royal theology of 2 Sam. 7:11b and in the ideas found in royal psalms—e.g., Psalms 2, 45, 78, 89, 110.

12. Prophetic oracles play a part in a number of liturgies recorded in Psalms. For additional reading on the matter, see S. Mowinckel, *Psalmenstudien* (Kristiania: Jacob Dytwad, 1921–24), 3:9–10, 30ff.; idem, *The Psalms in Israel's Worship,* trans. D. R. Ap-Thomas (Nashville: Abingdon Press, 1962); A. R. Johnson, *The Cultic Prophet and Israel's Psalmody* (Cardiff: Univ. of Wales Press, 1979); and J. Gordon Harris, "Prophetic Oracles in the Psalter" (diss., Southern Baptist Theological Seminary, Louisville, Ky., 1970).

13. Sociologically these alternate prophetic groups resemble members of a peripheral possession cult and may have consisted of individuals from the periphery of society. See Wilson, *Prophecy and Society*, 202–6.

14. Though Elijah generally appears in Kings as a solitary figure, his relationship with Elisha indicates that he also presided over a community of disciples as their "father" (2 Kings 2:3–12).

15. In Semitic languages the expression "sons of" often indicates membership in a group or guild. This title is used in Ephraimite narratives about prophetic groups in Israel during the reigns of Ahab, Ahaziah, and Joram (1 Kings 20:35; 2 Kings 2:3, 5, 7, 15; 4:1, 38; 5:22; 6:1; 9:1). Cf. Wilson, *Prophecy and Society*, 140–41.

16. Elisha kisses his father and mother out of respect and love, kills his oxen for a feast to take away any thoughts of returning, and leaves everything to follow his new parent Elijah. Similarities exist between this community of prophets and that of Jesus and his disciples described in the Synoptic Gospels.

17. Erhard Gerstenberger stresses the clan or familial origin of tribal wisdom and the "so-called apodictic" law, in *Wesen und Herkunft des "Apodiktischen Rechts"* (Assen, Netherlands: Neukirchener Verlag, 1965), 117–48.

18. Cf. Robert Gordis, *Poets, Prophets, and Sages: Essays in Biblical Interpretation* (Bloomington: Indiana Univ. Press, 1971), 160–97; Glendon E. Bryce, *A Legacy of Wisdom* (Lewisburg, Pa.: Bucknell Univ. Press, 1979), 150ff.; and Brian W. Kovacs, "Is There a Class-Ethic in Proverbs?" in *Essays on Old Testament Ethics*, ed. J. L. Crenshaw and Willis Crenshaw (New York: KTAV, 1974), 173–87.

19. The role of parents and grandparents in religious instruction also is stated in Deut. 6:7, 20–25; 11:19. For a discussion of wisdom and instruction, consult William McKane, *Proverbs: A New Approach*, Old Testament Library (Philadelphia: Westminster Press, 1970), 6–10; and R. N. Whybray, *The Intellectual Tradition in the Old Testament*, BZAW 135 (Berlin: Walter de Gruyter, 1974), 6–43. The phraseology "father" and "son," like "mother," must at times be understood literally as referring to family members. Evidence for professional teachers and pupils in Israel, in contrast to Egypt, points away from the existence of such schools until a late period. See Whybray, *Intellectual Tradition*, 42–43; and R. deVaux, *Ancient Israel*, vol. 1 (New York: McGraw-Hill, 1965), 48–50.

20. Much uncertainty surrounds this section. According to the passage, Agur may stem from the same area as Lemuel, perhaps a northern Arabian locality. But such an assumption depends on a tentative translation of *hammassaʾ*. Discussion of the unity of the passage and its difficulties can be found in C. C. Torrey, "Proverbs, Chapter 30," *JBL* 72 (1954): 95; and McKane, *Proverbs*, 643–57. Cf. R. B. Y. Scott (*Proverbs, Ecclesiastes*, Anchor Bible [Garden City, N.Y.: Doubleday & Co., 1965]), who organizes the passage as

(1) the challenge of the skeptic Agur (vv. 1–4); (2) an answer by an orthodox believer (vv. 5–6); (3) an appended prayer (vv. 7–9).

21. Cf. D. W. Thomas, "A Note on *lyqht* in Prov. xxx.17," *JTS* n.s. 13 (1941):154–55. The second translation comes out of reading *lahqat* for the obscure *liqqhat* of the MT.

22. "Young eagles" is a possible translation. Ravens and vultures are birds of carrion as in the *lex talionis*.

23. "Awe" or "respect" for the Lord is used in the Hebrew Scriptures in numerous contexts and with varying intensity. For additional reading on this phrase, see Scott, *Proverbs, Ecclesiastes*, 37; G. von Rad, *Wisdom in Israel* (Nashville: Abingdon Press, 1972), 53–73; and James L. Crenshaw, *Old Testament Wisdom: An Introduction* (Atlanta: John Knox Press, 1981), 91–96. Commitment to God enables a person to acquire wisdom.

24. The role of vv. 10–11 in chap. 9 is fiercely debated, with varying conclusions. One view concludes that vv. 10–12 continue the invitation of Wisdom found in vv. 5–6 and conclude chaps. 1—9 (cf. Scott, *Proverbs, Ecclesiastes*, 76). Another approach views vv. 7–12 as an interruption to the original address in vv. 1–6, 13–18 (cf. McKane, *Proverbs*, 368–69). McKane argues that the fear of Yahweh is not an original constituent of wisdom in Prov. 9:10 and 1:1–7. The emphasis represents a shift from education to piety, from submission to the teacher's discipline to reverence for God. For a view to the contrary, see von Rad, *Wisdom*, 61–69.

25. The format resembles that found in Egyptian instructional literature where kings tutor others. Cf. *Ptah-hotep, Merikare,* and *Amenemhat* (*ANET*, 412–19). *Massa'* could reflect the name of a northern Arabian tribe (cf. Gen. 25:14; 1 Chron. 1:30) or could indicate a place in Edom (Eliphaz the Temanite, in Job). Cf. McKane, *Proverbs*, 407.

CHAPTER 4. THREATS TO THE COMMON
THEOLOGY OF AGING

1. Adele Berlin points out three categories of characters in biblical narratives: (1) the round or full-fledged character, (2) the flat character or type, and (3) the functionary or agent. See Berlin's *Politics and Interpretation of Biblical Narrative* (Sheffield: Almond Press, 1983), 23ff.

2. Even in the later twentieth century only about five percent of the over-65 population—or about one million persons—live in long-term-care facilities. Residents in nursing homes are primarily the very elderly, with seventy-four percent being 75 years of age or older. The majority of older persons do not require hospitalization in the course of a year. See Charles S. Harris, *Fact Book on Aging: A Profile of America's Older Population* (Washington, D.C.: National Council on Aging, 1978–79), 126–28.

3. Responses to the rebuilding of the temple recorded in Ezra and Haggai may also reflect later negative priestly reactions to the second temple, as well as a glorification of the Solomonic temple by the Chronicler.

4. A related modern misconception assumes that the elderly rarely desire

intimacy in their relationships. Note the findings of a Consumers Union survey of older Americans, in *Love, Sex, and Aging,* ed. Edward M. Brecher (Boston: Little, Brown & Co, 1984), 18–27. Nursing-home rules and practices often seem insensitive to the sexual needs of residents. Even husbands and wives are assigned separate beds and rooms. Little privacy exists for them together. John Hendricks and C. David Hendricks (*Aging in Mass Society: Myths and Realities,* 2d ed. [Cambridge, Mass.: Winthrop Pubs., 1981], 350–58) discuss the misconceptions on which such policies may be based.

5. Other examples of this misconception appear in the narrative about the Shunammite woman (2 Kings 4:14–17) and in the Lukan account of the announcement of John's birth (Luke 1:7, 18).

6. The purpose of placing Abishag in bed with the king may have been to convey the health and heat of a young body to that of the ailing king. On the other hand, Abishag later appears to have been accepted as one of David's harem, and therefore Solomon resents Adonijah's request for her (1 Kings 2:13–25). Probably the beautiful young maiden was a test of the virility of the king. Ancient people felt that the well-being of the country depended on the virility of the king. If David were unable to pass this crucial exam, then he would appear unable to govern and a coregent would need to be appointed. See John Gray, *I and II Kings,* Old Testament Library (Philadelphia: Westminster Press, 1963), ad loc. Also, remember that the sickness of Keret in the Ras Shamra material seemed to disqualify him from reigning. Cf, *ANET,* 147–49; and John Gray, *The KRT Text in the Literature of Ras Shamra: A Social Myth of Ancient Canaan,* 2d ed. (Leiden: E. J. Brill, 1964), 2.

7. Recent laboratory surveys of workers point out that instead of being helpless and useless, older workers are, on the whole, absent less often than younger workers, but that the length of an absence because of illness increases with age. Some occupational adjustments could make it possible for the older worker to perform well on the job with relatively good health. See Sven Forssman, "Occupational Health and Old Age," in *Processes of Aging: Social and Psychological Perspectives,* 2 vols., ed. R. H. Williams, C. Tibbitts, and W. Donahue (New York: Atherton Press, 1963), 2:339–48. Additional information appears in both volumes concerning all aspects of the health of the older person.

8. The order of the traditions in Genesis seems to imply that Abraham also remarried by marrying Keturah (Gen. 25:1–4). These materials may be out of order chronologically to focus on Sarah and Isaac. The present context of the text suggests, however, that popular opinion considered Abraham's marriage and the birth of sons, even in his old age, perfectly normal and acceptable.

9. In today's world the term "dementia" refers to a broad class of diseases of the brain in which cells progressively and irreversibly deteriorate. Dementia affects from five to ten percent of the population over the age of 65; the

proportion rises to twenty-five percent for those 80 and over. The most common cause of dementia is Alzheimer's disease. Since there is no cure or effective treatment for the patient, family members and care givers especially need emotional support and physical relief from the stress of coping with the ill patient. See Lissa Robins Kapust and Sandra Weintraub, "Living with a Family Member Suffering from Alzheimer's Disease," in *Helping Patients and Their Families Cope with Medical Problems,* ed. Howard B. Roback (San Francisco: Jossey-Bass, 1984), 453–80. For further study consult the bibliography on pp. 479–80 of that book.

10. See G. E. Mendenhall, "The Relation of the Individual to Political Society in Ancient Israel," in *Biblical Studies in Memory of H. C. Alleman,* ed. J. M. Myers (Locust Valley, N.Y.: J. J. Augustin, 1960), 89–108; idem, *The Tenth Generation* (Baltimore: Johns Hopkins Univ. Press, 1973), 122–41; idem, "Social Organization in Early Israel," in *Magnalia Dei: The Mighty Acts of God,* ed. F. M. Cross, W. E. Lemke, and P. D. Miller (Garden City, N.Y.: Doubleday & Co., 1976), 132–48; and Edward Neufeld, "The Emergence of a Royal Urban Society in Ancient Israel," *HUCA* 31 (1960): 31–53.

11. The substantive "elder," *zaqen,* has the same form as the adjective meaning "old" and is formed from the root of the verb "growing old." It appears to be a derivative of the feminine noun *zaqan,* "chin," "lower jaw," or "beard." Hence the most obvious sign of the elder male is a beard. Cf. BDB, 278–79. The noun describes both a mature adult and a position of leadership. The verb *zqnu* appears also in Old Aramaic but only in reference to "being old." Hebrew is unique in using this noun as a term for elders. The noun *laheqah* appears as a collective term for elders, which corresponds with a similar root in Ethiopic. Cf. *TDOT* 4:122–31.

12. The most common reference to "elders" is "elders of Israel." Elders' functions fall into five areas: (1) they represent the entire people or a community at political or religious events; (2) they accompany or work with a leader as that person leads the community; (3) they act as a governing body or assembly with some authority to make decisions; (4) they participate in the royal council (2 Sam. 17:4, 15; 1 Kings 20:7ff.); (5) they render judgments as a judicial body (Deut. 19:12; 21:3, 19; 22:15; 25:1; Josh. 24:4; Ezra 10:14). Cf. John L. McKensie, "The Elders in the Old Testament," *Biblica* 40 (1959): 522–27.

13. Cf. Norman K. Gottwald, *The Hebrew Bible: A Socio-literary Introduction* (Philadelphia: Fortress Press, 1985), 286–325.

14. See Hanoch Reviv, *The Elders in Ancient Israel: A Study of a Biblical Institution,* Texts S (Jerusalem: Magnes Press, 1983). Hebrew monarchy failed to integrate organically with the old conservative patterns. Wealth concentrated more among wealthy urban business leaders. The money economy was disastrous for small landowners. Smaller agricultural communities and villages kept alive the role of the elders, the old system of property, the right of the family, and the system of kinship. Parallel to the royal administra-

tion, the old clan and local tribal councils survived until revived after the destruction of the monarchy. See Neufeld, "Emergence of a Royal Urban Society"; and idem, "Prohibitions against Loans at Interest in Ancient Hebrew Laws," *HUCA* 26 (1955): 355–412.

15. R. H. Charles, ed., *The Apocrypha and Pseudepigrapha of the Old Testament in English* (London: Oxford Univ. Press, 1913), 1:242–67.

16. See Moses Hadas, *The Third and Fourth Books of Maccabees: Jewish Apocryphal Literature*, Dropsie College ed. (New York: Harper & Bros., 1953), 36–39; and Charles, ed., *Apocrypha and Pseudepigrapha* 1:155–73.

17. Hadas, *Third and Fourth Books of Maccabees*, 54–55.

18. Ibid., 168–71; and Charles, ed., *Apocrypha and Pseudepigrapha* 2:653–85.

19. Hadas, *Third and Fourth Books of Maccabees*, 178–79.

20. Ibid., 184–85.

21. Ibid., 188–231.

22. This poem probably is not to be interpreted as an allegory of old age. The storm pertains to death, the real enemy of life. Unfortunately, the resulting breaking-apart of the body or house concerns the elderly directly. Old age always faces the specter of death as its greatest enemy. See Aarre Lauha, *Kohelet*, Biblischer Kommentar: Altes Testament (Neukirchen-Vluyn: Neukirchener Verlag, 1978), 209–15; Christian D. Ginsburg, *The Song of Songs and Coheleth*, Library of Biblical Studies (New York: KTAV, 1970), 458–69; and John F. A. Sawyer, "The Ruined House in Ecclesiastes 12: A Reconstruction of the Original Parable," *JBL* (1975): 519–31.

23. Cf. translation of this text with that in *The Five Megilloth and Jonah*, 2d rev. ed., intro. H. L. Ginsberg (Philadelphia: Jewish Pub. Soc. of America, 1974), 76–77.

CHAPTER 5. ISRAEL'S VARIATIONS ON
THE COMMON THEOLOGY

1. E.g., Amos 2:6; 4:1; 5:7; 11–15; 5:24; 6:12; 8:4–5; Isa. 1:23; 3:13–14; 5:23; 10:2; Micah 6:8. Though Proverbs often seems unconcerned about the needs of the poor (e.g., Prov. 14:20; 22:2) and views poverty as the result of laziness (e.g., Prov. 6:6–11; 28:19), still some sayings bristle with divine indignation over various forms of oppression of the weak (e.g., Prov. 14:31; 22:22–23; 23:10–11; 28:20–21). Also note Job 31:19–20. Cf. Johannes Pedersen, *Israel: Its Life and Culture*, 2 vols. (London: Oxford Univ. Press, 1926), 2:355–56, 410 (= [New York: Harper & Row, 1962–65], 2:129–87).

2. See Walther Zimmerli, "Ich bin Jahwe," in *Geschichte und Altes Testament*, Beiträge zur historischen Theologie 16, Albrecht Alt zum 70, Geburtstag dargebracht (Tübingen: J. C. B. Mohr [Paul Siebeck], 1953), 179–209; and its English translation in Zimmerli's volume of essays *I Am Yahweh*, trans. D. W. Stott, ed. Walter Brueggemann (Atlanta: John Knox Press, 1982). A full statement of this thesis, with a bibliography, may be found in Walther Zimmerli, *Old Testament Theology in Outline*, trans. David

E. Green (Atlanta: John Knox Press, 1978), 20–21. This formulaic self-introduction both expresses the majesty of Yahweh and protects the freedom of God to pronounce judgment on the acts of the people.

3. Since this law is one of only two positive commandments in the Decalogue, several efforts have been made to reconstruct its more primitive form. The reconstruction assumes that all the commandments were originally negative, apodictic statements. Some scholars view the earliest form of the Fifth/Sixth Commandment as "Thou shalt not curse thy father or thy mother," or "Thou shalt not despise thy father or thy mother." See the discussion in Eduard Nielsen, *The Ten Commandments in New Perspective,* Studies in Biblical Theology 7 (London: SCM Press, 1968), 78–86. Brevard S. Childs (*The Book of Exodus,* Old Testament Library [Philadelphia: Westminster Press, 1974], 394–401) argues to the contrary that the "juxtaposition of positive and negative laws in a series" remains characteristic of Old Testament law. He finds no historical priority of the negative.

4. The commandment would be misinterpreted if it were assumed to be one for keeping little children respectful of their elders. Instead, young adults are instructed to take care of parents in their time of feebleness. See Walter Harrelson, *The Ten Commandments and Human Rights,* Overtures to Biblical Theology (Philadelphia: Fortress Press, 1980), 92–105; and Martin Noth, *Exodus: A Commentary,* trans. John Bowden, Old Testament Library (Philadelphia: Westminster Press, 1962), 165.

5. The phrase "on the ground which Yahweh your God gives you" is wholly Deuteronomistic in style (e.g., Deut. 4:26, 40; 5:30; 6:2; 11:9; 17:20; 22:7; 25:15; 30:18). Expressions such as "that your days may be long" have an entirely separate history. Such express the common theology of the Orient as appears in certain royal psalms (e.g., Pss. 9:16; 21:4). This is a constantly recurring theme in Phoenician psalms. See Nielsen, *Ten Commandments,* 103–4.

6. The reversal of the order of mother and father in the LXX could represent the original reading. On the basis of accepting the unusual reading as the preferred one, however, evidence leans more toward the MT reading as the earliest. Perhaps the passage indicates some loosening of the older kinship arrangements. Cf. Noth, *Exodus,* 140.

7. The phrase "my sabbaths" and the plural "sabbaths" generally occur in the Holiness Code and in Ezekiel (e.g., Ezek. 22:8, 26; 23:38). The brevity of this commandment assumes the established nature of this observance. Cf. J. Morgenstern, "Sabbath," in *IDB,* 4:138–39.

8. See Joseph Reider, *The Book of Wisdom: Jewish Apocryphal Literature,* Dropsie College ed. (New York: Harper & Bros., 1957), 65. For the translation and discussion of the Wisdom of Solomon, see R. H. Charles, ed., *The Apocrypha and Pseudepigrapha of the Old Testament in English* (London: Oxford Univ. Press, 1913), 1:538–41.

9. R. A. F. Mackensie, *Sirach,* Old Testament Message (Wilmington,

Del.: Michael Glazier, 1983), 32–33; and Charles, ed., *Apocrypha and Pseudepigrapha* 1:323–25. For an introduction to the book, see Mackensie, *Sirach,* 13–18. Cf. Asher Finkel, "Aging: The Jewish Perspective," in *Aging: Spiritual Perspectives,* ed. Francis V. Tiso (Lake Worth, Fla.: Sunday Pubs., 1982), 121.

10. See F. Zimmermann, *The Book of Tobit: Jewish Apocryphal Literature,* Dropsie College ed. (New York: Harper & Bros., 1958), 62–65; and Charles, ed., *Apocrypha and Pseudepigrapha* 1:174–241.

11. Sons-in-law under some conditions should treat and respond to parents-in-law as "those who begat" the son (10:12).

12. The book has been preserved in Syriac, Arabic, Armenian, and other languages. The discovery of fragments in Old Aramaic (5th cent. B.C.E.) in the Elephantine Papyri has revolutionized how this popular folk tale has been viewed. There may have been an original Assyrian version of the work, but the Western world knows the story through its inclusion in the Arabian *Thousand and One Nights.* The Book of Tobit (2d cent. B.C.E.) is familiar with the story of Aḥikar. The fables of Aesop may have been drawn from the character. Cf. S. Sandmel, "Ahikar," and E. G. Kraeling, "Ahikar, Book of," both in *IDB* 1:68–69.

13. The Armenian version reads, "Son love the father who begat you and earn not the curses of your father and mother; to the end that you may enjoy the prosperity of your own sons" (Charles, ed., *Apocrypha and Pseudepigrapha* 2:732).

14. Also note the Armenian version and the lack of respect Nadan shows for his uncle (ibid., 740).

15. See ibid., 739. Also note the message that Aḥikar delivers to Nadan in 8.7 of the Arabic version. In the speech, Aḥikar compares Nadan to a fruitless tree that must be cut down (8.30). After the speech, Nadan swells until he bursts and dies. So will others experience destruction, the story implies, who do not respect and learn from their aging teachers (8.30 Arabic).

16. Cf. this vision with the one found in the Book of Consolation (Jer. 31:12).

17. Charles, ed., *Apocrypha and Pseudepigrapha* 2:214, 236.

18. The date of around 200 B.C.E. has been given to the book primarily on the basis of the eleven Aramaic manuscripts of *Enoch* discovered at Qumran. Fragments were also found of the Book of Jubilees and columns of the Genesis Apocryphon. Cf. J. T. Milik, *The Books of Enoch: Aramaic Fragments at Qumran Cave 4* (Oxford: At the Clarendon Press, 1976). Much more can now be said about the influence of *1 Enoch* on the rest of apocalyptic literature. See, e.g., James C. Vander Kam, *Enoch and the Growth of an Apocalyptic Tradition,* CBQ Monograph Series 16 (Washington, D.C.: Catholic Biblical Assn. of America, 1984).

19. Cf. *1 Enoch* 56.7, 99.5, 100.2 (Charles, ed., *Apocrypha and Pseude-*

pigrapha 2:270–71 [100]; and James H. Charlesworth, ed., *The Old Testament Pseudepigrapha*, vol. 1 [Garden City, N.Y.: Doubleday & Co., 1983], 39, 80–81).

20. Cf. Dan. 12:1–7.

CHAPTER 6. TWO RESPONSES TO RESPECT FOR THE ELDERLY

1. The Peloponnesian War of the late 5th cent. B.C.E. broke up these older, local kingship groups. Cf. W. K. Lacey, *The Family in Classical Greece* (London: Thames & Hudson, 1962), 25–29; and W. K. C. Guthrie, *The Greeks and Their Gods* (London: Methuen & Co., 1950), 300. But though the Athenians in theory respected and honored the old, actions hardly fit the theory. See James Hastings, ed., *Encyclopaedia of Religion and Ethics* (New York: Charles Scribner's Sons, 1925), 470–71. The enfeebling of the powers of enjoyment was viewed as a horrible state that lowered one to a living death.

2. Some softening of this law took place in the later Roman Empire as new laws likewise elevated and protected the mother. See E. Sachers, "Patria Potestas," in *Realenzyklopädie der Klassischen Alteriumswissenschaft*, ed. A. Pauly, and G. Wissowa (1953) 22/1:1046–1175; *Brockhaus Enzyklopädie* (1972), 14:302; and M. Kaser, *Das Römische Privatrecht* (1955–59), 2:142–45.

3. See Frank Stagg, *The Bible Speaks on Aging* (Nashville: Broadman Press, 1981), 153–54. Note esp. Gal. 3:28 and Col. 3:11 for examples of Paul's principles concerning racism and sexism. Paul omits any reference to the unity of all generations.

4. See John G. Gager (*Kingdom and Community: The Social World of Early Christianity* [Englewood Cliffs, N.J.: Prentice-Hall, 1975], 20–37), who posits that earliest Christianity took the form of a millenarian movement. He points out how the movement meets the five criteria of a cult and yet, unlike most cults, survived beyond a normal brief life span to become a historical movement.

5. Luke expands Mark's reference to the popular rumor that Jesus was one of the prophets (Mark 6:15) by adding the phrase "a certain of the ancients," *archaion* (Luke 9:8). Yet neither this venerable title nor the perception that Jesus was John the Baptist *redivivus* explains to his satisfaction the nature of Jesus' task. But Luke more than Mark recognizes that two "ancient" powers and messages are clashing in the ministry of Jesus.

6. Matthew more than Mark does not disassociate Jesus from the law and the prophets. Instead, Jesus represents the ultimate fulfillment of the Scripture and is the supreme follower of the ancient law despite the fact that the tenets represent only interim instructions (Matt. 5:17–20).

7. This enigmatic text reads, "And no one having drunk the old (*palaion*) desires new (wine); for that one says: the old (*palaios*) is good" (Luke 5:39).

8. For a discussion of the structural features of the 1st-cent. Mediterranean

kinship system, see Bruce J. Malina, *The New Testament World: Insights from Cultural Anthropology* (Atlanta: John Knox Press, 1981), 96–102.

9. Groups attracted to this millenarian movement would yearn for a criticism of the old and a vision of the new such as a prophet might offer. Jesus' rejection of established criteria like wealth and kinship ties as means to measure human worth implies that the members of this new community were outsiders of the social and religious system. Cf. Gager, *Kingdom and Community*, 22–33.

10. See Gerd Theissen, *Sociology of Early Palestinian Christianity*, trans. John Bowden (Philadelphia: Fortress Press, 1978), 8–16. Theissen isolates the characteristics of the so-called wandering charismatics as (1) homelessness, (2) lack of family, (3) lack of possessions, and (4) lack of protection.

11. Q emphasizes the radical nature of discipleship even more than Mark does. In the Markan tradition, Jesus' family thinks he is mad (Mark 3:21, 31) and he has to leave his hometown (Mark 6:1–6). Still Q states that even routine family responsibilities are to be ignored in order to announce the imminence of God's kingdom (Luke 9:59–62; 14:26). See Richard G. Edwards, *A Theology of Q* (Philadelphia: Fortress Press, 1976), 127–28; and Howard Clark Kee, *Understanding the New Testament*, 4th ed. (Englewood Cliffs, N.J.: Prentice-Hall, 1983), 86–89.

12. See Malina, *New Testament World*, 94–116, for information on the defensive kinship and marriage strategies of the era.

13. Practice in early synagogues indicates that most elders had attained some measure of seniority before assuming the office. The exact composition of this group remains largely obscure. Often the Bible uses the term *presbyteroi* as a title for an official rather than as a designation of age. No doubt Christians borrowed the word from the Greek translation of the Old Testament (LXX), and its primary meaning is "old person" (e.g., in Luke 1:18; Philem. 9). See A. E. Harvey, "Elders," *JTS* n.s. 25 (1974): 319–27.

14. E.g., the parable of the prodigal son describes a younger brother who finds happiness in the house of the father while the elder brother remains isolated outside the house (Luke 15:25). Though the term "elder" generally means older, the parable also may utilize the word to refer to those who follow the traditions of the elders.

15. See G. Bornkamm, in *Theological Word Book of the New Testament* 6:662–63. Despite the popular viewpoint of Lightfoot, it remains doubtful that Christian presbyters ever organized themselves into any formal or official body after the mode of an existing Jewish institution. They remained too informal to demand a chairman who eventually would become a bishop. See Harvey, "Elders," 323–26.

16. Local synagogue elders had almost no responsibility for worship leadership; the task was reserved for the head of the synagogue. Older, aristocratic members must have formed a local administrative or judicial council to deal with issues concerning the life of the community (Harvey, "Elders,"

324–25). Elders ranked after priests in importance to the Qumran community. Twelve laymen or elders served on the council of the community. Elders studied two years and then passed through a two-year probation for moral testing before being fully approved. For additional information on elders in Qumran, see the "Manual of Discipline," IQ 1:19–21; 6:4, 8; 8:1. Cf. Theodor H. Gaster, *The Scriptures of the Dead Sea Sect* (London: Secker & Warburg, 1957), 58, 64–65, 67; A. R. C. Leaney, *The Rule of Qumran and Its Meaning* (Philadelphia: Westminster Press, 1966), 187–88; P. Warnberg-Moller, *The Manual of Discipline, Translated and Annotated with an Introduction* (Grand Rapids: Wm. B. Eerdmans, 1957), 30; and William Hugh Brownlee, "The Dead Sea Manual of Discipline: Translation and Notes," *Bulletin of the American Schools of Oriental Research* supp. studies 10–12 (1951): 8, 10–11, 24.

17. Such lists are called *Haustafeln* by Luther. For a complete bibliography on the subject and an explanation of the issues involved in current studies, see D. Schroeder, "Lists, Ethical," in *IDBSup*, 546–47; and Peter T. O'Brien, *Colossians, Philemon*, Word Biblical Commentary (Waco, Tex.: Word Books, 1982), 214–20. New Testament scholars remain divided over the exact origin of such house tables. No doubt they also serve as a Christian apology addressing concerns of outsiders. See Abraham J. Malherbe, *Social Aspects of Early Christianity*, 2d ed. (Philadelphia: Fortress Press, 1983), 50–53.

18. Malherbe, *Social Aspects*, 50–53; and Wolfgang Schrage, "Zur Ethik der Neutestamentlichen Haustafeln," *New Testament Studies* 21 (1974): 1–22.

19. Against Edward Lohse, *Colossians and Philemon*, trans. W. R. Poehlmann and R. J. Karris, Hermeneia (Philadelphia: Fortress Press, 1971), 158–59.

20. For a complete description of the more advanced eldership system described in the postapostolic writings, see Bornkamm, in *Theological Word Book of the New Testament* 6:672–80; and Harvey, "Elders," 329–32. A good example of that developed system appears within the *First Epistle of Clement to the Corinthians* 44–58. Clement from Rome expresses his alarm at the ejection of several faithful elders in Corinth. He criticizes the ouster and defends the leaders as "blameless" and "honorable" (chap. 44). In chap. 47 he calls "disgraceful" and "perverted" the sedition against certain elders of Corinth. Therefore he calls the people to submit to their elders in true humility and repentance (chap. 57) and to reestablish peace and harmony (chap. 58). Cf. A. Cleveland Coxe, *The Apostolic Fathers with Justin Martyr and Irenaeus* (Buffalo: Christian Literature Pub. Co., 1886), 17–21; W. K. L. Clarke, ed., *The First Epistle of Clement to the Corinthians* (New York: Macmillan Co., 1937), 72–82; and Ludwig Schopp and Bernard M. Peebles, eds., *The Fathers of the Church: A New Translation*, vol. 1 (Washington, D.C.: Catholic Univ. of America Press, 1969), 43–58.

21. See Malina, *New Testament World*, 116–17.

22. First Peter employed a current household concept to achieve order, concord, and solidarity for the Christian community as the "household of God." See John H. Elliott, *A Home for the Homeless: A Sociological Exegesis of 1 Peter, Its Situation and Strategy* (Philadelphia: Fortress Press, 1981), 165, 233. Elliott (pp. 215–16) argues that the *Haustafel* form is not used in 1 Peter as an apology and has little specifically in common with the treatise of Josephus. This is against Malherbe (*Social Aspects*, 52–53), who argues that the *Haustafeln* form was employed in 1 Peter to counter charges that Christianity was antisocial.

23. Raymond E. Brown (*The Gospel according to John, 1—12*, Anchor Bible [Garden City, N.Y.: Doubleday & Co., 1966], 98–111; and *The Community of the Beloved Disciple* [New York: Paulist Press, 1979], 192–95) views the rebuke as a Johannine addition to the text made in order to harmonize it with the Synoptic picture. Nevertheless, the positive view of the mother of Jesus fits the normative family picture recorded in the rest of the Gospel.

24. Unfaithful Christians and the Jews seem to be the most severe opponents of John's community, not the family or the traditions of the elders. See Brown, *Community*, 59–91, esp. 88–91; and R. Alan Culpepper, *The Johannine School* (Missoula, Mont.: Scholars Press, 1975), 278–86.

25. During Jesus' lifetime, chief priests and members of the Sanhedrin opposed Jesus. John uses the more inclusive term to include these groups and to refer also to the Jews who later expelled Christians from their synagogues, thus leaving them without any official protection against the "Roman inquisitors" (Brown, *Community*, 40–43).

26. This once-independent passage, John 7:53—8:11, represents an early Christian tradition that found its way into the Fourth Gospel and some manuscripts of Luke after 21:38. Cf. Brown, *The Gospel according to John*, 335–38, for a full discussion of its canonical and textual problems. Some textual witnesses add the phrase "unto the last" (KJV). Though this passage is not Johannine in origin, it agrees with the Gospel of John's more positive view of aging and elders. Nevertheless, it naturally fits in the historical context of Luke 21:38.

27. See Bornkamm, in *Theological Word Book of the New Testament* 6:668–69.

28. Cf. *Pirke Avoth* (Sayings of the fathers) 1.1 (R. H. Charles, ed., *The Apocrypha and Pseudepigrapha of the Old Testament in English* [London: Oxford Univ. Press, 1913], 2:691). Contrary to this tradition, scholars recognize that the Mishnah contains a body of judicial interpretations accumulated through many generations which emerged in a form called *halakhah*. Some of the traditions may have begun with Ezra, but nameless teachers increased the number and complexity of the *halakhot*, until an orderly arrangement was accomplished that was termed the Mishnah. See Charles, ed., *Apocrypha and Pseudepigrapha* 2:686–87, as well as additional works introducing the Mishnah and Talmud.

29. Cf. Passover Hagaddah and Berakhot 1.5 (*The Mishnah*, trans. Herbert Danby [London: Oxford Univ. Press, 1933], 3). See also Benjamin Blech, "Judaism and Gerontology," in *Aging and the Human Spirit*, ed. Carol LeFevre and Perry LeFevre (Chicago: Exploration Press, 1981), 11.

30. See *Encyclopedia Judaica* 11:848.

31. Two collections exist, the Babylonian and Palestinian Talmuds. They include *Gemara* for some of the tractates of the Mishnah. The collections are the result of years of study within rabbinical schools. Decisions in religious law are rendered first on the basis of the Babylonian Talmud. Only when the Babylonian Talmud does not oppose the Palestinian Talmud would the latter be followed. See Hermann L. Strack, *Introduction to the Talmud and Midrash* (1931; New York: Meridian Books, 1959), 65–72.

32. Charles F. Horne, ed., *Medieval Hebrew: The Sacred Books and Early Literature of the East*, vol. 4 (New York: Parke, Austin, and Lipscomb, 1917), 122.

33. *P. Pe 'ah* 15c (A. Cohen, *Everyman's Talmud* [New York: E. P. Dutton & Co., 1949], 183).

34. Horne, ed., *Medieval Hebrew*, 122.

35. For a thorough study of the child's obligation to parents, see Gerald Blidstein, *Honor Thy Father and Mother: Filial Responsibility in Jewish Laws and Ethics* (New York: KTAV, 1975), 63–74.

36. *Kiddushin, Seder Nashim*, vol. 4, trans. H. Freedman, in *The Babylonian Talmud*, ed. I. Epstein (London: Soncino Press, 1961), 151; and Blidstein, *Honor Thy Father and Mother*, 45.

37. Though books of Haggadah (scriptural interpretation that is non-halakhic) appeared as early as the 3d cent. C.E., pure haggadic midrashim date from later. Assembling of the material continued until 1040 C.E. and even beyond (see Strack, *Introduction*, 201–5).

38. See Blidstein, *Honor Thy Father and Mother*, 51–115, for a more extensive discussion of the Midrash (p. 52) and the issues raised on parental support.

39. Historical Jewish perspectives on aging are discussed in Asher Finkel, "Aging: The Jewish Perspective," in *Aging: Spiritual Perspectives*, ed. Francis V. Tiso (Lake Worth, Fla.: Sunday Pubs., 1982), 111–34. Other comments on modern practices and perspectives appear in Blech, "Judaism and Gerontology," 4–20. Note also a guide for volunteers, describing forty-eight programs of help for the aging by Jewish women (*Continuing Choices: A Comprehensive Handbook of Programs for Work with Older Adults* [New York: National Council of Jewish Women, 1975]), and a pamphlet by Abraham Heschel (*To Grow in Wisdom* [New York: Synagogue Council of America, 1961]). The synagogue has long promoted a reverent attitude toward the old. See Newman M. Biller, "The Role of the Synagogue in Work with Old People," *Jewish Social Services Quarterly* 28 (1952): 284–89.

SCRIPTURE INDEX

AUTHOR INDEX